Teaching and Learning in Real Time: Media, Technologies and Language Acquisition

Carla Meskill
Professor, Educational theory and Practice
University at Albany
cmeskill@uamail.albany.edu
(518) 442-5007

© 2009 Athelstan

Athelstan
5925 Kirby Drive
Suite E 464
Houston TX 77005

info@athel.com

TABLE OF CONTENTS

1. Instructional Media & Technology and Language Learning: An Overview 1
   - SECOND LANGUAGE TEACHING AND LEARNING: A FRAMEWORK 8
   - SUMMARY 10
   - COMING TO TERMS 11
   - WHERE WE HAVE BEEN 13
   - Activities 19
2. *The Media* as a Second Language 21
   - MEDIA CHARACTERISTICS 23
   - ON CULTURE 24
   - IN THE CLASSROOM 29
   - COMMERCIALISM AND CRITICAL VIEWING 33
   - SUMMARY 34
   - Activities 34
3. Principled Uses of Media and Technologies 39
   - COMMUNICATIVE LANGUAGE TEACHING 39
   - COMMUNICATIVE LANGUAGE TEACHING, MEDIA, AND TECHNOLOGY 43
   - DESIGNING MEDIATED LANGUAGE LEARNING ACTIVITIES: THE CHUNQUING TOOL 51
   - THE CHOREOGRAPHY OF MEDIATED LANGUAGE LEARNING ACTIVITIES 57
   - SUMMARY 63
   - Activities 63
4. The Aural: Talking About, Around, & Through Audio Technologies 67
   - LISTENING 68
   - THE ROLE OF THE AURAL IN LANGUAGE TEACHING AND LEARNING 69
   - AUTHENTIC VS. REPURPOSED VS. COMMERCIALLY PRODUCED AUDIO MATERIALS 78
   - AUDIO LABS: BEYOND THE BOOTH 81
   - AUDIO: BEYOND THE CLASSROOM 85
   - SUMMARY 86
5. The Visual: The *Why and How* 89
   - USING VIDEO IN THE CLASSROOM 102
   - VIDEO IN CLASS AND OUT 105
   - CLOSED CAPTIONING 107
   - COMPREHENSIBILITY VS. AUTHENTICITY 107
   - SUMMARY 108

END OF CHAPTER NOTE: EXPLOITING THE MEDIUM 108
Activities 109

6. Computers in Language Learning: From Constructed to Constructing 113
COMPUTERS AND LEARNING: A BRIEF HISTORY 115
COMPUTER ASSISTED LANGUAGE LEARNING (CALL) SOFTWARE 117
WHAT COMPUTERS CAN AND CAN'T "DO" 121
CLT AND COMPUTERS 122
CRAFTING CONTEXTS OF USE 123
SUMMARY 128
Activities 129
APPENDIX—FOR MORE INFORMATION ON CALL: 136

7. Computer Communication Tools 139
COMPUTERS AND WRITING 140
TELECOMMUNICATING AS A SECOND LANGUAGE 143
SYNCHRONOUS WRITTEN COMMUNICATION 147
DISTANCE LEARNING 151
SOME SOCIOCULTURAL CONSEQUENCES OF ONLINE LEARNING 154
SOME CONCEPTUAL GUIDELINES 157
SUMMARY 158
Activities 158
APPENDIX: FOR FURTHER READING AND INFORMATION 161

8. Multimedia: Spaces, Performances, and Characters 163
OPPORTUNITIES FOR L2 COMMUNICATION 164
MULTIMEDIATED COMMUNICATION 169
THE CONE OF INSTRUCTION 170
ANALOGOUS SPACES 171
MULTIMEDIATED LISTENING 174
SUMMARY 177
Activities 177
APPENDIX: RESOURCES FOR LISTENING MATERIALS ON THE WEB 180

9. Electronic Literacy as a Second Language 181
LITERACIES 181
FORM 184
E-TEXTING 186
MODELS AND SCAFFOLDS 192
SUMMARY 194
Activities 194

Epilogue 199

References 201
Subject Index 209

References 201
Subject index 205

Preface

With the widespread infusion of media and technologies in learning institutions around the world, there is a call for teacher guidance in practical, pedagogically grounded ways to make optimal uses of tools old and new. Colleges and universities are responding to this need both by offering courses specific to language and technology and/or by incorporating media and technology issues in language teaching methodology courses. This text is designed for use in both contexts. The framing of media and technology uses within current thinking about how language is best learned is its central concern. *Real Time* is designed for language professionals: pre-service, in-service, and teacher educators. It can serve as a course text for teacher preparation courses, professional development activities, and as a reference for advanced work in media and technologies studies.

The text is about the art and craft of teaching and learning language when images, audio, video, telecommunications, The Media, and multimedia are integrated into instructional processes and used as tools for successful, motivated learning. It is a comprehensive guide and resource for foreign language, second language, language arts, and bilingual teaching professionals. Readers are guided to consider/reconsider media and instructional technologies as tools for socially mediated learning with students and teachers actively engaged in acquisition-rich discourse and activity. This perspective sees media and technology serving as springboards and catalysts for active, hands-on language learning and teaching.

Real Time's chapters are organized around specific technologies: images, audio, video, telecommunications, computers in instruction, and multimedia. The first three chapters present and discuss principles for understanding and undertaking tools-based instruction, while the final chapter explores the nature and significance of "electronic literacy" as it impacts second language learning.

For the past eighteen years I have had the privilege to work with numerous, highly motivated and dedicated language professionals on the issues explored in this book. Together we fabricated, assembled, banged on, and broke all manner of software and hardware in our quest to assess their teaching and learning potential. This text represents the many and diverse conceptual bumps and breakthroughs we made together through collaborative discussions (online and off), develop-ment activities, evaluation projects, classroom implementations, and research. It is my pleasure and privilege to share what I have learned in the hopes that readers will be able to benefit from the conceptual groundwork we found necessary for the effective use of media and technologies in language education.

Carla Meskill
University at Albany
December 2, 2001

Note Regarding Updates

When *Real Time* was originally published in 2002, the goal was to make it as timeless a text as possible. As much as was realistic at the time, I tried to avoid treatment of specific technologies as the word on the street was that these were going to change. And change they did.

The emphasis of the text remains on the conceptual work needed to employ media and technologies thoughtfully and well in language pedagogy. With the assistance and technological wizardry of Jason Vickers, *Real Time* now reflects both technological changes as well as changes that Jason's students have reported would enhance their learning about media and technology in language education.

We hope this new version suits the needs of students, teachers and scholars of language pedagogy with media and technologies.

Carla Meskill
University at Albany, State University of New York
March, 2009

1. Instructional Media & Technology and Language Learning: An Overview

> *If a new mind is arriving, then it is one in which perspective is everything.*
>
> (GUYER, 1999)

Free-flowing, accessible data. Images, information, control. What do these features of our electronic era spell for language instruction? Teachers of all subject areas in all parts of the world are pondering this question—those who have been actively integrating media and technologies in their teaching, and those who have not yet begun to do so. Many teachers and students who have been enjoying these tools, the richness and great mileage they bring to learning, have seen media and technology expanding their notions of what it is to teach and to learn. The benefits of using media and technology along, with understanding the anatomy and purposes of instructional practices in tandem with such tools are central themes in this text. Throughout these chapters you are encouraged to explore the coming together of what we currently understand about learning additional languages, the attributes of media and technology, and good practices for language education.

Media and technologies can be tremendously useful tools for extending the ways both learners and teachers consider language learning enterprises and for generating fresh and stimulating perspectives. However, it is the position of this text that such new perspectives are not simply born out of the physical presence of wires and electrodes. On the contrary, it is our forever flexible and evolving beliefs about how language is best taught and learned that serve as the most critical groundings to further the evolution in our thinking about, with, and through these new tools.

In one way or another, all media and technology involve human communication. As such, language is at the heart of the medium and the messages represented by, and transmitted through the various devices and materials discussed in this text. In addition to what we know about language and language learning processes, understanding the attributes of media and technologies can take us to new places in the conceptualization of teaching and learning.

LANGUAGE AND LANGUAGE LEARNING

> *I was never knocked out. I've been unconscious, but it's always been on my feet.*
>
> FLOYD PATTERSON, former heavyweight boxing champion of the world
> (Remnick, 1999)

The Problem of Language. As long as humankind has been able to communicate, the nature and origin of the signs and symbols of that activity have been the source of a fleet of questions and conundrums. How is it that we humans can get our meanings across in so many diverse and inconsistent ways? When the patterns of our communication *are* consistent across time, culture, and languages (e.g., syntax), how does that happen? And what about two personages from recent history—former heavyweight boxing champion Floyd Patterson and the character Ray Babbitt, played by Dustin Hoffman in the movie *Rainman*?

Floyd Patterson

Former heavyweight champion of the world, Floyd Patterson (an African-American) took the title from Archie Moore (a White American) in 1956. His victory was a devastating blow to racist boxing aficionados. Patterson eventually lost the title to a young upstart named Cassius Clay, further altering the profile of professional boxing in the twentieth century. In his twilight years, Patterson's infamy as former champion landed him a desk job. In 1995, New York governor George Pataki appointed Patterson head of the New York State Athletic Commission, a position that called on him to do very little. Up until 1998, that is. That year he was called to give a deposition on questionable boxing promoter practices. It was at that hearing that the impact of Patterson's sixty-four professional bouts and countless knockdowns became clear. Here is an excerpt from the trial (taken from Remnick, 1999):

Q: Who did you fight [for the heavyweight title in 1956]?

P: I'd have to think about that...I can't remember the opponent I fought, but I wound up beating him to become heavyweight champion of the world.

Q: Where did the fight take place?

P: I really don't know. I think it was in New York...

Q: Do you know the name of your predecessor, chairman of the New York State Athletic Commission?

P: Yes, I do know, but, uh, I didn't get that much sleep last night to tell you the truth and I am very, very tired and it's hard to think when I'm tired.

Q: What's the secretary's name?

P: Oh boy. I see her quite often. I know her well. I just forget the name...

After so many thunderous blows to the head, Patterson had become what is known in boxing circles as 'punch drunk.' The manner in which this excessive battering manifested itself in Patterson's cognitive abilities is clear: he was unable to recall the most memorable and salient aspects of his life—the bout that won him the championship title, names of people with whom he had had extensive daily contact. What is striking about Patterson, and why he is included in a discussion of the problems associated with language, is that his syntactic and semantic ability is intact. Not only that, but the sociolinguistic competence he demonstrates in this passage is impeccable – something that would surely be the envy of learners of English as a second language. He is incredibly adept at responding in socioculturally appropriate ways to his inquisitor. He hedges, punts, avoids, and literally dances around the questions put to him. His compensatory strategies reveal that, apart from his memory, something in his brain—language ability—is ticking along quite efficiently.

A common occupational hazard for boxers had taken hold of Patterson's memory abilities. Although he displays sociolinguistic finesse, his ability to recall facts is absent. His language, but not his memory, is intact and highly functional.

Ray Babbitt

In 1988, Dustin Hoffman won an academy award for his brilliant portrayal of Ray Babbitt, an autistic savant. This character represents an interesting contrast to Floyd Patterson's memory deficit and accompanying intact language ability. Unlike Patterson, Babbitt's memory is supremely intact while his sociolinguistic competence is absent. Ray has an uncanny ability to recall an extraordinary number of facts: e.g., baseball statistics, dates and times of events, tens of thousands of strangers' names and phone numbers. He recalls all sorts of information that, unfortunately for his contacts with others in the world, is thoroughly trivial and irrelevant to managing day-to-day existence. Like most autistics he is unable to connect with others in communication—neither through the language or content he uses, nor non-verbally. (A common characteristic across autistics is the inability to make eye contact and to backchannel—give verbal and nonverbal feedback—with others.) As is reflected in the following dialogue, Ray's sociolinguistic competence is nil.

Here his brother, played by Tom Cruise, is trying desperately to carry on a conversation. In this scene, he has just kidnapped his brother from the institution in which he has spent most of his life. He is just beginning to learn about Ray's deficits and his special abilities. The night before, when Ray became agitated about having no books to read, he ends up reading the telephone directory and just prior to this dialogue rattles off the phone number of the waitress serving them in a restaurant (*Rainman*, 1988):

> C: How'd you do that? Did you memorize the whole book?
> R: No.
> C: The beginning?
> R: Yes.
> C: How far you'd get?
> R: G.
> C: G? Godsakes.
> R: Yea, Godsake, William, William and Marsha Godsake.
> C: A, B, C, D, E, F, G?
> R: Yes.
> C: That's good Ray.
> R: Yea.
> C: I like that.
> R: Yea.
> [There's a bit of silence]
>
> C: Well, you hungry?
> R: Tuesday we have pancakes.
> C: Pancakes?
> R: Yea.
> C: Well that sounds good.
> R: With maple syrup.
> C: You bet your butt.
> R: You bet your butt.
> R: Uh-oh.

C: They got pancakes.
R: Where is…where is.
C: What is it Ray?
R: Uh-oh, of course I don't have my toothpicks.

Where Babbitt's memory is hyperacute, his sociolinguistic ability is greatly impaired. Patterson's sociolinguistic ability is intact, his memory is impaired.

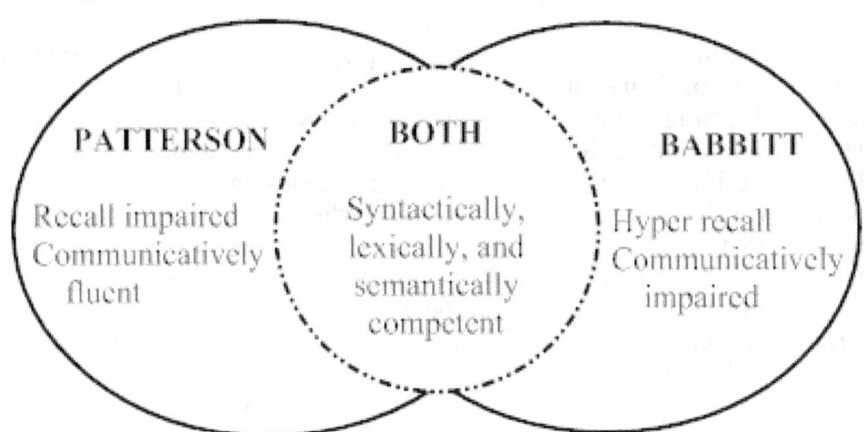

Note that in both cases these fellows' syntax and semantics remain flawless. Like Floyd Patterson, Ray Babbitt speaks in syntactically well-formed sentences. Unlike Patterson, however, he is not engaging in the kind of shared meaning-making that characterizes human communication. He does have, unlike Patterson, an uncanny facility with recall and sharp sensory abilities. If you'll recall, later in the film he goes on to demonstrate these amazing memory abilities at a Las Vegas casino.

And so…?

You are most likely saying to yourself, *what have these two anomalies got to do with learning language?* The Floyd Patterson–Ray Babbitt contrast is illustrative of the memory/cognition versus linguistic competence conundrum. We ask learners to 'learn' language in the classic sense; that is through study, memorization, and recall. As this one example demonstrates, there is something more and more complex going on in the brain besides recalling words and stringing them together into sentences.

Recent understandings about language indicate that communication happens not in the head of the individual nor as an act of transmission from one individual's head to another's. Rather, communication is currently conceived as the merger of utterances in the spaces between speakers. It is there that meaning gets negotiated and constructed. In the cases of Patterson and Babbitt, we can see what happens when partial physiological capacity to communicate is impaired. We can also surmise from these cases that even when memory is greatly impaired, the ability to be sociolinguistically successful remains viable and where memory is acutely functional, sociolinguistic competence may not function well at all.

There can be any number of physiological impairments to communication. What makes these two cases intriguing for second language learning is the fact that their composite seems to indicate that memory and communicative ability appear to be startlingly separate phenomena. For the field of second language learning, the implications of this are twofold. First, it can give us pause when considering instructional practices that rely on students' memory in their learning. And second, it makes us reconsider the sociolinguistic dimension of second language learning and how it may indeed be less memory dependent than our instructional practices reflect. Furthermore, the contrast of these two cases may be indicative of learner differences in terms of the individual contribution of memory versus sociolinguistic predispositions.

LANGUAGE LEARNING

Recent thought in the field of second language learning to a great extent parallels that of broader postmodern thought. We have moved away from the general belief that thought—its genesis and evolution—was strictly in the head. Likewise there is dissent with the parallel notion that learning an additional language is simply comprised of getting the proper raw material into the head of a learner. Recent conceptions of language learning processes have broadened 'out of the head' and developed into ways of understanding human cognition that are chiefly social; that is, thought (and language) are socially mediated with central development being manifest in discourse constructed between and among people. This manner of thinking and talking about language learning falls under the broad, general rubric of *sociocognitive* or *ecological*[1] views of learning (van Lier, 2000).

---

[1] van Lier (2000, p.259) defines the term *ecological linguistics* as seeing language "as the totality of linguistic activities and relationships among

Slow to Change…

We still somewhat unwittingly adhere to myths about language, about learning, about communication, about memory. A number of lay concepts about language learning have been culturally shaped by such myths as:

> the memorization myth
> the intelligence myth
> the talent myth

That there is some direct connection between one's ability to memorize and one's ability to learn additional languages is a long-held belief. The Patterson-Babbitt examples heartily rattle these mythical foundations as do countless personal experiences of language learners whose attempts to master a new language through the memorization of words and structures have resulted in abject failure (see, especially, the discussion in Oller, 1978). Even those who have remarkable memories report that learning a language well, so one can fully function in it, is much more than memorization. Likewise, it involves much more than tests of intelligence can predict. Many an 'uneducated' person (a.k.a., folks who would perform dismally on tests of intelligence) master additional languages without a hitch.

Myths about having a special 'talent' or 'ear' for language are similar to myths about intelligence overall in that they are born of flawed notions, but are nonetheless stuck in our talk and concepts. The error lies in the belief that one comes to the task of learning equipped with certain mental skills and abilities and that these in turn *cause* success. This has formed the basis for the tradition of abilities testing done in advance of any *instructional experiences* where we now understand the locus of learning to reside (Resnick, 1999). This assessment practice has both fueled the misconception of innate abilities and, in teaching practices, skewed learner achievement; e.g., if one's abilities-assessments indicate strengths or weaknesses, this is then reflected, however subtly, in expectations about, and treatment of learners. The self-fulfilling prophecy of the test-abilities-before-learning tradition has perpetuated the myths of special talents and intelligence, especially for learning language. In many corners, there's long been movement away from these myths and, consequently, their influences in guiding theory, research and practice have dissipated to some degree. However, you need only ask yourself and those closest to you about these myths to realize their tenacity.

---

speakers and between speakers and the physical, social, personal, cultural, and historical world they live in."

Second Language Teaching and Learning: A Framework

The following heuristic forms the backdrop for the proceeding chapters in this text. It is a conceptual aid that helps communicate the current ecological state of affairs in the second language acquisition field, and one that has also served others in the development of many materials and media/technology-based activities for language teaching and learning.

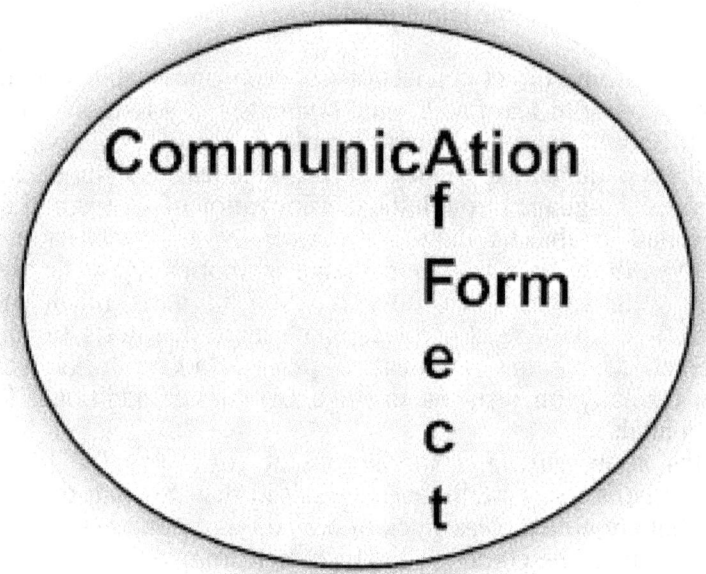

The oval above represents the interplay of three essential concerns in the teaching and learning of additional languages: Communication, Form, and Affect. The first portion, Communication, has received a great deal of press both within language and its related disciplines and throughout other non-related disciplines as well (e.g., new emphases with math, science social studies, etc. on learners' mastery of the discourse of those disciplines—both spoken and written). In the language profession, communication or 'communicative competence' has been a cornerstone of theory, research, and practice over the past forty-odd years. In part this communicative movement is in reaction to early beliefs about and approaches to language learning that saw the process as consisting of the memorization of discrete pieces of language through repetition with little or no focus on meaningful use of the target language. Emphasis on Communication is also due to fundamental changes in the conception of language that were brought about by the Chomskian revolution in the nineteen sixties (Chomsky, 1986). Language was no longer viewed as a knowledge set external to the individual, but as a biological endowment or predisposition that allowed humans to generate an infinite quantity of novel utterances. This capacity for creativity, in conjunction with an explosion of research on child first language acquisition brought to the language teaching community fresh views of the learner as active agent, as having a first or native language that was an asset rather than a liability, and has having a predisposition for acquiring additional language through active use, rather than passive reception.

Independent of Chomsky's reframing of the language and language acquisition issues is the current popularity of Lev Vygotsky, a Soviet learning psychologist whose writings from the early part of the twentieth century are frequently cited in contemporary research across disciplines. One of Vygotsky's major claims centers on the critical role of discourse in learning (Vygotsky, 1986). Communication between learners and more capable others provides a linguistic 'leg up' in cognitive development. This notion of Communication being the locus of learning has permeated a great deal of work in the late twentieth and early twenty-first centuries. In terms of *this* heuristic, Communication is conceived as the central locus of second and foreign language acquisition. It is through using the language under study that one masters its various components and ultimately becomes 'communicatively competent'; that is, being able to communicate what one wishes in the right way, at the right time, under the right conditions with the desired effect (Hymes, 1972).

The second aspect of this conceptual frame is Form. Out of four decades of concentrating on the communicative, we have learned that this alone is not sufficient for learners to be successful. Rather, an eclectic balance of communicative practice with ongoing attention to form is desirable. Ideally, learners' attention is drawn to Form in such a way that they are continually *aware* of the way the target language they are using operates.

Finally, there is the component Affect. This term encompasses a range of large, overarching sociocultural issues such as context, emotion, personhood, and motivation (local and intrinsic). This complex of interdependent factors is critical in understanding the ways learners succeed and don't succeed in acquiring a new language. Numerous recent studies involving ethnographic approaches aimed at examining this broad, complex construct underline the importance of *self* in contexts with others in understanding learning in general, and language learning in particular. One's sense of self, and the affective states a particular context or activity provoke, continually change. Changing states determine varying levels of receptivity to others, to information, and to learning (Schumann, 1997). Recall that both Patterson and Babbitt were under great duress in the above examples: Patterson on the witness stand, Babbitt the victim of a kidnapping. In addition to, and sometimes despite our skills and abilities, how and what we communicate is tied to the intricate nature of our immediate environments and our emotional relationship to them. We never communicate in a vacuum. Contextual factors interact with, and indeed determine affective change. This, in turn, impacts how and what we understand and communicate. It also greatly determines our receptiveness, and thus our successes, in learning another language which is very risky business in terms of Affect.

Like all learning activity, activity with media and technology requires grounded conceptions of the interrelated factors that influence learning. As a simple heuristic, Communication, Form, and Affect, provide a foundation upon which we will consider media and technologies use in language learning. At the center is the learning process conducted by human actors who operate as a community (**Affect**) where individuals actively participate (**Communication**) while attending to what is being learned (**Form**). It is through engagement in such contexts and activity that second language acquisition can be successfully nurtured. The essential ingredients for such contexts are: opportunities for learners to learn (**C**); a focus for learning (**F**); and deeply personal reasons—a personal investment—when using the language (**A**).

SUMMARY

In its forty-year history, the field of second language acquisition has bustled with theoretical and empirical activity. The field has made progress in establishing itself as a viable and respected discipline of its own, and has made advances in articulating its own mission. While almost the same age, the field of instructional technology has not enjoyed the revolutionizing conceptual changes that the field of Second Language Acquisition (SLA) has. Or, if it has, it has been very indirect (e.g., the development of more sophisticated interfaces has made the business of computers child's play with a resulting indirect impact on education). The interplay of our current understandings at the juncture of second language learning and instructional technologies are therefore somewhat parallel. We understand the essential nature of how another language is acquired and have some limited empirical evidence to support this. We understand some essential components of learning with and through media and technology with similarly extant, but by no means conclusive empirical evidence to support this. In both cases, the complexity of process—learning language and learning with technologies—is unruly in terms of present research methodologies. Capturing the intricacies and complexities of human processes in both regards represents a continuing challenge. As far as practice is concerned, the following chapters attempt to instantiate what is understandable from these two fields at this juncture through scenarios, case studies, and practical information and examples of language teaching and of learning with media and technology.

COMING TO TERMS

Before we begin this exploration, here are the ways key terms are used in this text:

> **language learning**—*acquiring the linguistic skills and competencies needed to operate in a language other than one's native language, both formally through instruction, and informally through interaction within target language environments*
>
> **mediation**— *activity around something in the middle position. v.t.,* **mediate**
>
> **technology**—*(from the Greek 'technologia,' systematic treatment of an art) a scientific method of achieving a practical purpose; in contemporary terms – machines enabling and supporting human activity*
>
> **The Media** – *(originated 50 years ago from field of advertising) a channel or system of communication, information, or entertainment; a mode of artistic expression or communication; agencies of "mass communication"*

In the last decade, the notion of technology and The Media have converged. Television, newspapers, and magazines in digital form are now considered 'technology'. Even in their non-digital form, these media have also begun to take on the attributes of their internet counterparts; that is, television screens, along with newspaper and magazine layouts and genres have come to greatly resemble internet screens and vice versa. For our purposes both the terms technology and The Media refer to the "stuff" that we use to support or *mediate* instruction: this includes everything from chalk, to desktop publishing; from felt boards to 3-D graphics generators; from a teacher's voice to a multimedia simulation.

What concerns us is not so much a generic term for this 'stuff', but ways in which they get *used* – the roles they actually play, in teaching and learning.

In the chapters that follow, the term *mediate* describes *the middle position* and implies that things in that middle position are being used to assist or *mediate* the learning. Mediation implies that there are learners (usually more than one) and/or a teacher positioned in relation *to the medium in the middle*. It also implies that language – the target language – is being actively instructed, practiced, and learned. In the figure below, the thing in the middle is being referred to, talked about, and manipulated by learners in consort with their teacher and the goals and activity she has designed; it is *mediating* the learning. Productive use of the target language is mediated, facilitated, and supported by the activity with the medium mediating the language instruction the teacher designs and orchestrates around it.

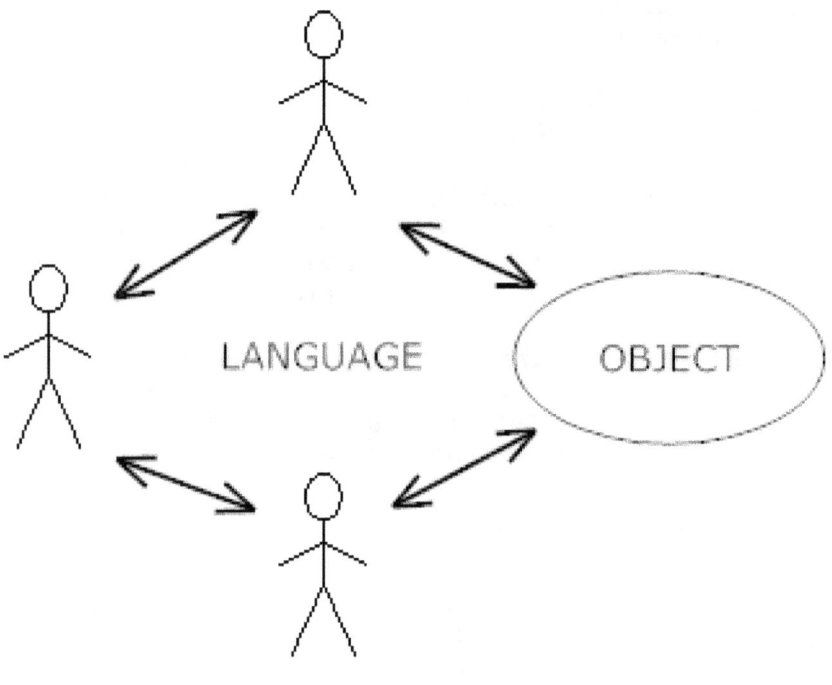

"Mediated" Learning

The *technology* of this instructional object is comprised of its formal, physical characteristics: paper, ink, layout, font, digital files, connectivity. As you read this page, however, the substance and meaning get *mediated* by your skill, prior knowledge, and level of interest in the topic. It is a *medium* in that the symbols on the page require mediation between mind and object. Further, if a concept or illustration on this page became the focus of a conversation with a colleague, the object becomes a *medium* of communication and learning. The way mediation is used here in this text reflects historical shifts in how we have thought about language learning and the tools used to affect it.

Note that with the addition of "the," as in *The Media*, the term becomes one that refers to "mass media"—newspapers, magazines, radio, TV, and the like. The term *The Media* will be used accordingly.

WHERE WE HAVE BEEN

Teaching and learning have always been mediated in some fashion or another. From the most ancient forms of instruction mediated by stick drawings in the dirt, to the most sophisticated multimedia telecommunications of today, technologies have served learning in a variety of ways. Indeed, since the beginning of recorded history, beliefs about, and practices in language learning and the use of objects in language instruction have gone through a series of interesting changes, changes that reflect beliefs about how language is best learned or acquired.

Throughout the ages, great numbers of people have successfully learned additional languages readily and well without formal instruction—no classrooms, no course books, no Berlitz tapes, no Rosetta Stone, not even dictionaries. People who accomplish this make use of their immediate environments, including any appropriated tools (objects, symbols), to acquire the words and structures they need to communicate. From street children of Sao Paolo to merchants in Tibet, more often than not, additional languages get "picked up" naturally without formal instruction. Travel, commerce, imperialism, and marriage are some situations that motivate and necessitate the acquisition of new means for communicating.

In ancient Rome, "natural" routes to acquisition made up only one half of the picture. Privileged families believed their offspring could pick up quite a bit of a second language (Greek) in the home by *using* it in quotidian interactions around the home. For these offspring of the upper classes, their initial second language learning experiences, like their first, were thus *mediated* by the immediate environment. Servants, tutors, and family members spoke Greek with the child throughout the course of the day. This extended experience with communicating and understanding the second language prepared them for the more systematic modes of second language learning they would later encounter in school. Once of school age, children raised bilingually came to their formal schooling experiences prepared to engage in more *technology-*

oriented learning activity (e.g., grammars, slates, declensions, texts for recitation). We can speculate that this merger of the formal and informal constituted a balanced, eclectic mix of the mediated and the technological in second language learning. It combined the need for learners to experience the language in all its chaos (the environment) and as a systematized science of rules and lexicons. As we will see, such a balanced approach is now in favor within the language education profession.

Widespread use of the kinds of systematic written grammars common to Roman schooling continued through the Middle Ages. During this time the popularity of Greek faded and was replaced by the new lingua franca, Latin. Considered the language of logic and precision, Latin came to be instructed accordingly. Rigorous attention to the details of form ruled the day. Little attention was paid to comprehension, nor was there any productive use beyond parroted translations. In effect, the technology of formal instruction was emphasized at the exclusion of the *mediated*.

This is not to say that language learning only occurred in formal school environments. Outside of classrooms, missions, monasteries, and tutoring sessions whose practice was deeply rooted in the *science* of learning, languages (Latin especially) continued to be informally "picked up" as needed by the masses. Whereas the study of Latin was considered an enterprise that expanded one's mind and level of cultural sophistication, it was also the language of art and commerce.

Music, theater, and storytelling were both the principal forms of entertainment and the *mediums* by which languages were learned. Through emotional and intellectual involvement in the ethos of captivating artistic fictions, individuals could understand (with visual help) and internalize the meanings represented orally in a different language. Artists traveled from land to land to sing, dance, act, and tell engaging tales. These minstrels, troubadours, *comedia del arte* troupes and various other traveling artists performed in ways that made language difference irrelevant and understanding through involvement and personal response primary. At the same time, successful commerce between peoples depended on the ability of one or both parties to communicate either in the lingua franca of the day or in some creatively constructed creole or composite of the languages known to each.

In formal education, the tendency toward the scientific and technological continued into and through the Renaissance. The main objects that served as instructional tools were grammars, dictionaries, and instruments of writing. Some dissent to this scientific approach was, however, brewing. In the sixteenth century, Desidrius Erasmus, a Dutch intellectual, began questioning the rationale behind these rigid instructional practices. His main argument against them was that beyond training students to mimic and memorize, it was impossible for language to be internalized devoid of meaning and context. Authentic use, he argued, through activities such as reading, playing games, and interacting in the target language, was the surest route to proficiency in another language. Erasmus therefore advocated an emphasis on realistic use of language as central to instructional activities. Such activity could be supported, he contended, by using pictures and realia—*media*, according to our definition above. Language learning through meaning-ful practice could thereby be *mediated* by objects co-opted from everyday life for use in instruction.

Erasmus began what became a widely popular movement upon which many subsequent scholars and practitioners built heavily. Indeed, his work laid the foundation for a great deal of modern thought and steered development of language learning practices. His work is considered the precursor to what became the Natural Method (eighteenth century) and eventually the Direct Method or "eclectic method" (late nineteenth, early twentieth). Both the Natural and Direct methods saw fairly widespread acceptance outside the shrinking hard-core grammar translation tradition. Both the Natural and Direct methods, in keeping with what Erasmus had advocated, represent a trend toward the *media*ted in language instruction (Bowen, Madsen & Hilferty, 1985).

From the fifteenth through the early twentieth century, while "high" learning of Latin continued, an alternative instructional trend leaned more toward *mediated,* and less toward *technological,* forms of instructional practice. The objects that came to support instruction—pictures and everyday objects—were objects with which to think, and around which to make meaning. For the traditional study of foreign languages, the technology of grammars and translations persisted. With the turn of the nineteenth to the beginnings of the twenty-first century came a tremendous shift in the basis of western economies—a shift from agriculture to industry. In keeping with the rapid movement toward industrialization, education became an enterprise reconceived to match this broader socioeconomic transition. The manufacturing metaphor was quickly applied to what and how schools should teach. Like factories, schools should *produce products;* they needed to *equip* students with *skills;* classroom issues should be treated as *management* issues; teaching became *skills training;* and, to *administrations, efficiency* became paramount. Schools were perceived of and designed as *production lines* which *delivered* a standard, *quality-controlled end product* (an educated citizen) that could be *manufactured* with maximum *efficiency* and *uniformity.*

Within the industrial system of education, the role of the teacher is one of a purveyor of knowledge. This knowledge comes in standard sets that get conveyed into the minds of their charges. Students come to the learning enterprise a *tabula rasa*; the teacher's job is to fill that blank slate with knowledge sanctioned by those in power.

The industrial model views technologies (machines) as the ideal means of delivering knowledge. The role of technologies, then, like that of the teacher, became one of efficient knowledge transfer. Each advent of a new technology brought renewed faith in this proposition: radio, audio recordings, filmstrips, slides, projectors, and so on. Each was seen as a means of modernizing teaching and learning and, in turn, increasing uniformity and productivity (Cuban, 1986).

In the nineteen fifties, the work of psychologist Benjamin Skinner further fueled the popularity of the manufacturing metaphor. Based on the premise that all learners could be trained through operant conditioning, Skinner developed an instructional system known as Mastery Learning. Skinner's Teaching Machines—technologies that guaranteed uniform, individual mastery of content—were an immediate hit in the school-as-factory environment. Without teacher variability, *commodities* (educated students) could now be *delivered* with *uniform quality* (see, for example, Skinner, 1968).

With the industrial education complex came a radical shift away from mediation back to an even more rigid scientific set of beliefs and approaches to instruction, especially language instruction.

From Instructionism to Constructionism

Chances are at some time in your career as a student, a film projector, VCR or DVD player was wheeled into your classroom. The shades were drawn, the lights went out, and the unit was turned on. You sat quietly and watched along with your classmates. The purpose of this kind of technology encounter was for a set content to enter your head, much the same way content was to enter your head when the teacher lectured or drilled. The rate and efficiency with which this knowledge became imprinted on your brain was seen as superior to less reliable human interventions. There was, after all, no variation in content or in its presentation. Variability in teaching skill was eliminated as a confounding factor in the drive for product uniformity. Uniformity was in effect guaranteed by virtue of a consistent *transmission of the knowledge set*.

Such beliefs about and approaches to teaching and learning fall under the term *Instructionism*. In the field of language teaching, Instructionism is manifest in teaching methods such as the Audio Lingual Method (for complete description, see Richards and Rogers, 1989). Such methods were steered by the belief that students were passive *tabula raza* that got molded into learned beings (competent readers and writers of the target language) through the formation of good habits; e.g., one acquired the correct skills through memorization, drilling, and repetition.

Clearly our understandings about teaching and learning in general, and teaching and learning languages in particular, have since evolved a great deal. The last three decades have seen a distinct shift away from:

- student as passive recipient of knowledge
- teacher as purveyor of knowledge
- 'knowledge' determined by the powerful and the few
- media and technologies as efficiency machines,

toward:

- learners as active and central to learning processes
- teachers as designers and orchestrators of these processes
- knowledge locally and socially constructed by those invested
- media and technologies as support for the above

Learners are now perceived as central, the *sine qua non* of instructional endeavors. Their engagement in productive learning activity is the focus of instruction with the teacher's role one of designer, orchestrator, facilitator, and evaluator of learner tasks and activities. Technologies are perceived as *tools* to mediate and facilitate these processes.

Mediating learning with technologies—both simple and complex—requires a view that holds preeminent the individual learner, her unique qualities and the experiences she brings to learning. This is a view that casts the teacher in radically different and diverse roles, and that sees technologies as tools for active, productive learning rather than as purveyors or transmitters of skills and knowledge. Most importantly, it views the acquisition of skills and abilities as intrinsically social; that is, we learn language from using it productively in communication with others complemented by instruction in its forms and functions. Technologies, being primarily instruments of and for communication whereby attention to form and function can be highlighted and anchored, can be seen as ideal tools, then, for language learning and teaching.

For example, one minute a technology can serve as a source of information for students to negotiate and use productively. In the diagram below, learners access linguistic and cultural information on the web to be incorporated into a class project:

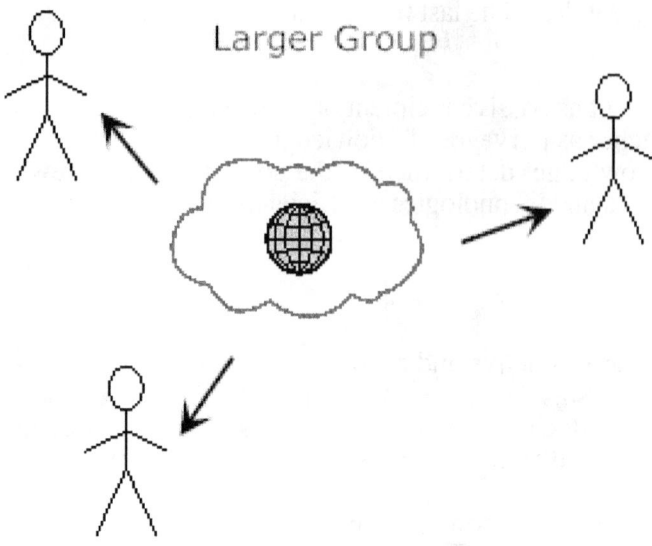

The next minute the medium serves as an object to talk around – as when learners discuss the design of a material packet they are assembling for their target language pen pals:

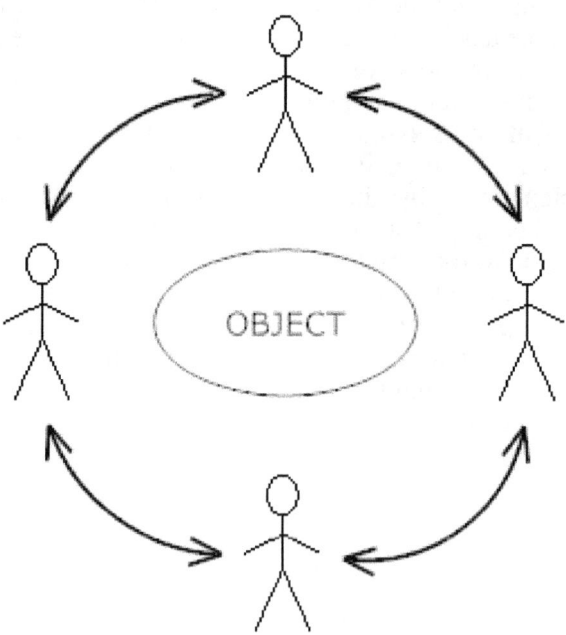

And the next, a tool to talk through – perhaps they query experts about social concerns in the target culture:

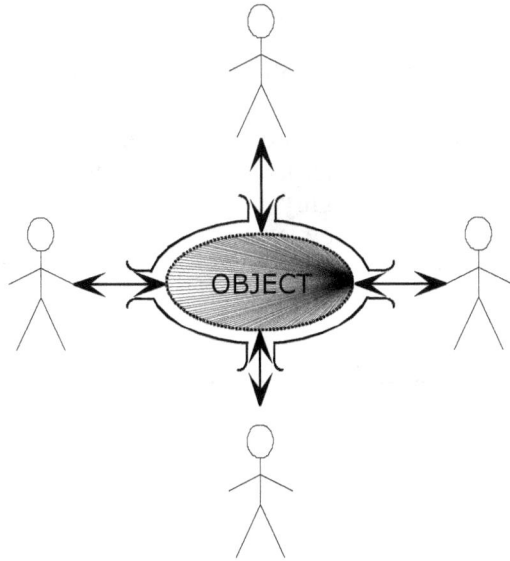

Today technologies are called into the service of instruction in a wide range of manners. Conceptualizations concerning intelligent uses of technologies tend to complement instructional approaches to language education, the CFA discussed earlier. The following chapter examines how contemporary learners of an additional language make use of The Media and how features of The Media can be exploited for powerful language instruction.

Activities

One Scenario

Select one instructional activity you recall engaging in while learning an additional language and do the following:

- Describe it.
- Locate the **C**ommunication and describe it.
- Locate the **F**orm and describe it.
- Locate the **A**ffect and describe it.

Using words, sketches, or both, describe your sense of the heuristic as it applied to this and other instructional activities in which you have participated.

MEDIA AND TECHNOLOGY: SUPPORTING ATTRIBUTES

Media and technology have a much to offer by way of support for language teaching practices. As perceptual objects they have both forms that can be referred to, and highly integrated meaning potential inherent within them. Come up with a few examples of audio and video in terms of their form-meaning correspondences that you have had direct experience with:

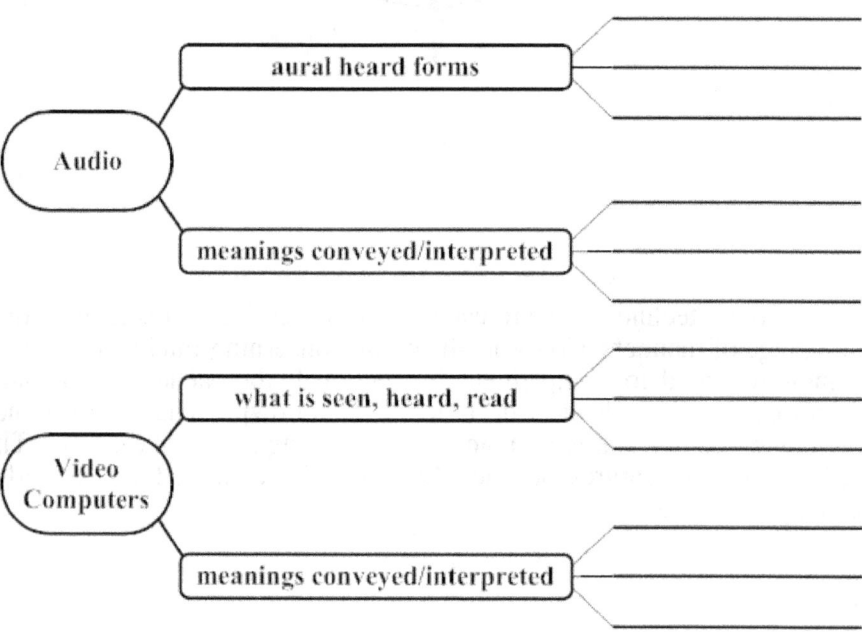

Review your own language learning experiences that have somehow been touched by these attributes. Brainstorm any influences these may have had on your own learning.

2. *The Media* as a Second Language

> *Television is above all a language that must be learned—a language whose influence is felt by all but which is taught by no one.*
> (Cohn, 1981, p.29)

> *It is not difficult to see that were language capable of producing material wealth, wind-bags would be the richest men on earth.*
> (Stalin, 1972, p. 35)

Every day, information pours into our ears and eyes though The Media. For many it has become such a presence that life would be startlingly empty without it. For many others, what is seen and heard on television and radio is as real as what goes on outside of the box. Actors and politicians wriggling through speakers and on screens carry more immediacy and seem more familiar than if they were physically in the same room. They are indeed *larger than life*. We are so accustomed to judging, believing, in short, *responding*, to what we hear on the radio and see on television to the point that this occupies a great deal of our conscious and unconscious lives.

There are two main schools of thought when it comes to The Media. One proclaims its destructive side and pushes for its eradication. The other school of thought maintains that understanding popular media —becoming media literate—is an absolute necessity if we are to be in control and not *be* controlled and manipulated by it. Both camps agree that television especially needs to be forcefully confronted by those who consume it. This is even more the case as radio, television, and electronic media crank up the pace, intensify messages, and compete more vigorously for our attention.

Some social pundits in the U.S. have long advocated for controlling the 'impact' of The Media through regulation of the message, not necessarily through the education of the reader and interpreter of the message. The Media is indeed a primary source of social models, social nurturance and, consequently, the shaping of our social identities; the danger is wholesale appropriation versus critical filtering of what one sees and hears (McLaren, Hammer, Sholle & Reilly, 1995; Rushkoff, 1996; Tyner, 1998). It is important to consider, however, that Bugs Bunny did not make a violent, irreverent generation; the larger sociopolitical forces that the show parodied and mocked, did.

In discussing the role of The Media in learning another language and culture, a healthy awareness of its motivations and mechanisms is advocated throughout this and subsequent chapters. We begin by examining the positive, supportive features of The Media in language education, then to some necessary qualifications and suggestions concerning the teaching of critical media literacy skills in tandem with language and culture.

INSTRUCTIONAL ATTRIBUTES

More than ever, the entertainment qualities of The Media are the most striking of its features. When corralled into the thoughtful language practitioner's tool chest, these entertainment qualities can be exploited to contribute a great deal of excitement, motivation, and relevance to language learning processes. In particular this can happen by virtue of The Media's capacity to:

1) render listeners/viewers into a relaxed, receptive state;
2) foster unpredictable links between what are otherwise disparate elements;
3) activate our drive to make sense, no matter what it is we see and hear;
4) broaden our view to include the opinions and interpretations of others;
5) be affectively powerful—The Media causes us to laugh, frown, fret, and cry.

In addition to being entertaining, The Media is dense in content. It therefore makes excellent material for developing content or theme-based language learning activities. Radio, TV, and Internet materials can easily be 'repurposed' for use in classroom and laboratory-based language instruction (see *Authentic Material* in Chapter 3 for a discussion concerning *repurposing*). Moreover, The Media can be exploited for richness of form, symbol systems, and genres. Television, Internet sites, and radio programming can be treated as 21st century texts to be deconstructed and explicated. By explicitly teaching critical media literacy skills, listening, viewing, and reading can be rendered active mediated encounters in lieu of passive "transmitted" intake, and as such have the potential for optimizing language acquisition opportunities.

Finally, the wealth of linguistic and cultural information packed into media presentations is enormous. There is a great deal of variation in communication styles and discourse patterns that more closely represents what goes on in the target culture. As such, The Media represents a way to closely study how language and culture are played out in a vast number of content realms. These "texts"—radio, television, and electronic media—are not only rich resources for understanding language and culture, but are materials that all students are interested in, motivated by, and quite accustomed to 'reading.'

MEDIA CHARACTERISTICS

Evocative
Popular media is, by nature, stimulating and evocative. It is aimed by design to provoke and manipulate our emotions. While this is potentially dangerous, the aspect of emotionality is nonetheless a feature than can act positively on the language learning process. It motivates sustained attending, it touches us deeply, it provokes us to make connections in our minds between its content and our own, real lives and experiences. It prompts us to suspend disbelief and become thoroughly engaged and even engrossed in its presentation. The Media tells stories with which we can gain perspective on the events and feelings of our lives and those of others.

Engaging
Earl Stevik is one language learning scholar who has long contended that depth of engagement with language is critical when learning that language (Stevik, 1976). The kind of engagement he refers to is that which takes place in the processes of meaningful and motivated communication with other human beings. When we are thoroughly engaged in the making and understanding of meaning, he proposes, we are in a state most conducive to language acquisition. We transcend the self-conscious learning mode and enter into activity that is directly aiding the internalization of the language we are using. The emotional dimension of media can induce a trance-like state of receptivity and depth of processing. When we are carried by plots and characters to a state of thorough engagement, our minds are particularly well tuned to understanding and, in turn, acquisition.

Structured
Television is a unique and powerful medium in terms of its visual dimension. The images that we see on the screen are carefully crafted to have very specific effects on our thoughts and emotions. There are a vast number of visual conventions in television programming that are reliably informative and evocative. These conventions, e.g., camera shots, editing techniques, and special effects, consequently supply viewers with a great deal of critical information that shapes their interpretations of and reactions to what they see on the screen. Viewers are also quite good at making use of the rich information supplied by the physical context in

which action takes place. Experienced film and television viewers (the vast majority of the world's population!) are adept at making use of these conventions to process and understand what they are watching. We can assume that our language students have had substantial experience with the various genres of film and television and that they are therefore equipped with certain "genre templates" they can employ with target-language media. Experience interpreting the visual conventions of drama, for example, results in mental schemata that viewers can apply to target-language viewing. In other words, if you've seen one soap opera, you've seen them all!

Extras
Movements, gestures, and facial expressions supply a great deal of information regarding "what's going on." Having your students watch a 30-second segment of a television show with the sound off is instructive in this regard. The visual information on the screen will most likely lead them to very on-target assumptions about plot, character, and ethos. Likewise, the music in drama and comedies indicates mood, foreshadows events, and underlines the unexpected. Sound mixing (e.g., crickets, wolf howls, and crowd noises) supplies additional information regarding ambiance and action. Finally, the perennial laugh tracks of sitcoms and comedy shows let us know when something funny has been said or has happened. In short, attributes of The Media align closely with **A**ffect in language learning and teaching.

ON CULTURE

My interest in non-native English speakers' perceptions of the language and culture of the United States, as seen through popular media, began in the early 1980s. I was teaching ESL to the first wave of Haitian 'boat people' in an adult evening program. There were several classes going on in the same building, all for men and women who spoke little or no English. About three weeks into the program, the director called all two hundred students and eight teachers into the school cafeteria. A large video monitor and VCR had been set up at the front of the room. The director explained in both Creole and English that he wanted everyone to see a film. He said no more, proceeded to press the play button, and left the building. The movie was *The Diary of Miss Jane Pittman,* the story of black slavery in the South. As the movie progressed, it was clear that the students could not engage the story line, most likely because they could not understand what the actors were saying. They began to talk among themselves, periodically glancing over at the screen. Soon, however, they abandoned their conversations. Their eyes became riveted to that screen where images of whites beating blacks screamed out. As the film genre is so well suited to do, the pain and humiliation of this treatment of blacks at the hands of larger-than-life white men provoked a reaction. Palpable ripples of agitation spread through the large room. Anger and confusion marked the buzz of the crowd. We implored one of the Haitian teachers to stop the movie and situate and explicate the story. She did this, but the crowd remained visibly distressed by the sounds and images they had experienced.

One can only imagine what thoughts and images those adults carried back to their homes that evening. Here they were, newly arrived in the United States. They had taken tremendous risks, uprooting their families from all that was "safe" and familiar. They did so to realize their dream of raising their families in this country. What had this movie conveyed about the country for which they had taken such risks? Had they understood the language, they may have been able to situate this brutality in its historical and geographic context. Even still, with or without the language that accompanied them, those images were powerful. In many ways these images resembled those that are continually pumped into the world's living rooms. Daily contact with images and language reflecting U.S. culture are impacting non-native speakers, but *how*?

Another early teaching experience also caused me to wonder about out-of-class encounters with popular media. As a brand new teacher of ESL, I can vividly recall my first adult education class. There was a mix of ages, nationalities, socioeconomic statuses, and levels of native language literacy and English language proficiency. I knew we needed to focus on people, topics, and issues that would motivate meaningful use of the language between and among us, but looking at these twenty-five work-weary faces, I wondered what knowledge about the world we all shared.

This group had worked and parented all day. The room was hot and close, and that depressing fluorescent lighting common to old public school buildings rendered their faces other-worldly. I had written a simple sentence on the board for which I had left the subject blank. I looked at their empty yet expectant faces and frantically searched my mind for a name for that blank. I wanted a name that would evoke recognition and interest—someone with whom all were familiar and that would induce a sense of solidarity through shared experience. I first mentioned the name of the current U.S. president and looked at them expectantly for signs of recognition. A few smiled and nodded. The rest either shook their heads or remained as before. Then I hit on what I thought would surely ring a bell. I wrote "Jesus" in the blank, pronounced it in English and in Spanish and again looked for recognition. About three quarters (the non-Asians) indicated recognition. I named a few other "universally" known public figures, each time getting a mixed review. Finally, and I believe it was somewhat jokingly, I said and wrote "Micky Mouse." Sparks of recognition ignited the entire group. They smiled at one another and nodded. We had discovered common ground.

Getting a sense of students' media habits and media literacy skills is an important aspect of assessing needs and in turn fashioning appropriate coursework. First, language learners bring media literacy skills to the task of learning language. Teachers can capitalize on these skills. Learners have had contact with radio, television, and films in their *native language*. For example, if you are accustomed to a musical refrain in your native language, you are equipped to recognize and make use of the same musical convention in understanding lyrics in another language. If you have spent hundreds of hours decoding the messages of advertisements on television and radio, you automatically transfer this skill to media in the target language. Most often, learners have spent a great deal of their lives employing listening and viewing strategies with The Media. They therefore come to the language classroom very skilled and proficient in using their knowledge about media genres and conventions to understand what they hear and view. These skills and strategies can be exercised in a number of ways.

Individual Viewing Habits

The Media practices of your students are likely to be as diverse as their individual backgrounds and personalities. After numerous interviews with non-native speakers in the United States, concerning their English-language media habits, I have found variation in preferences and patterns of contact, and also some instructive trends. In some situations where groups tend to be homogenous by age and native culture, commonalities are more likely. School-age children, for example, tend to watch the programs their native-speaking peers watch. This is chiefly due to scheduling and peer-generated interest; there are shows that are "cool" to watch and talk about, and there are those that are not. Likewise, there are topics in The Media for which certain groups are enthusiastic. Results of a large-scale media questionnaire for middle school students for whom English was not the first language, for example, revealed a common interest in sea life, sea mammals in particular. The same inquiry found that middle school children consistently favored afterschool reruns of situation comedies (Meskill, 1998). Like their native-speaker peers, they used these shows as models of dress, behavior, and language use.

For the most part, both adults and adolescents reported that they see their media contact time as an opportunity to practice listening to English while enjoying the programming and accessing information important to their daily lives (e.g., news, sports, local announcements, consumer information). Some reported purposely making use of this contact to improve their language skills. Others, who had not been aware they were doing so prior to being asked, also reported that this contact time had in fact been productive for language growth. Observations such as these are common: "TV helped me understand how emotions are expressed in the U.S." (Japanese male); "I truly learn and internalize best what is most personal to me" (Puerto Rican woman in the context of discussing her love of and involvement in English-language movies), and "Gestures and facial expressions [especially in dramatic shows] help me understand what speakers on TV are saying" (Meskill, 1996). Many have pointed to the motivating aspect of television: "I am motivated to work at understanding because so much information is missing from just the pictures on the screen." The majority see The Media as a way to be informed, entertained, and as a way to learn the target language. There were two exceptional cases: I call these the *insulationist* and the *studious* subgroups.

Media as Insulation: Too much of a good thing?

The following cases describe individuals who indeed made use of The Media to learn English, but also as an escape from more threatening encounters with the target language.

While living as a student in the United States, a Japanese woman reported that she had set up her living room as a high tech language lab. She had purchased a closed caption decoder for her big screen television and recorded shows with captions on her VCR. These she viewed over and over, stopping, rewinding, viewing portions again, and repeating what she heard out loud. This activity became her only English-language contact. In discussing her media-centered lifestyle, this young woman expressed the sense of safety she felt spending her days in this way. She felt she was being productive in her language learning and therefore justified in spending all of her time in seclusion. To her, the thought of going out into the English-speaking community was a fearful proposition. She reported that native speakers had a difficult time understanding her and were oftentimes rude. She was very aware of her need to learn English and, to her, this was the best way to go about it. Television represented a safer place for her to have contact with the country with which she was so intrigued.

Happily, the second "media junky" relied heavily on media only when she initially arrived in the United States. This reliance tapered off as her linguistic abilities improved and she consequently sought out forms of contact with language and culture beyond her television screen and, in this case, her radio. Recognizing her need to learn English quickly and well, this young woman kept her television on for most of the day, even when not watching it. She felt her language skills were benefiting from the talk emanating from the television even when she was doing other things. At night, when she finally turned the television off, she turned on the radio and fell asleep to talk shows and music in English. According to her, her fluency increased rapidly and with it her confidence to seek out additional opportunities to use the language. Without that initial "immersion" through television and radio, she states, she would not have been able to reach that level of confidence and proficiency. She needed to hear English twenty-four hours a day to internalize its sounds and cadences. She needed to study language in use and the cultural behaviors that accompanied it on the television. In this case, initial media immersion served as more of a jumpstart than as a refuge from native-speaker contact.

Another interesting case of intensive media contact was not brought about by a perceived need to learn English nor a desire to understand U.S. culture while living in it. It was, rather, the result of situational factors. Two Afghani housewives and mothers of small children were found to spend 6-8 hours a day watching daytime television. Their explanations for doing so are instructive. First, because they were Muslim, they were expected to stay home. Their husbands, their religious beliefs, and their cultural heritage dictated that their place was in the home, not among those whose beliefs and lifestyles were radically different from their own. Television viewing time, then, simply represented "something to do." The second reason they gave for this extended viewing practice was that the topics and format of daytime television—chiefly soap operas and talk shows—mirrored the kind of daytime activity they were accustomed to at home—that is, gossip and storytelling. Watching soaps and talk shows became surrogate activity for what they were used to doing in their native country. In Afghanistan, moreover, their media contact was primarily with Indian films—a genre characterized by romance, intrigue, and melodrama – not unlike U.S. soap operas and talk shows.

When these women were asked about the English language and U.S. culture they may be picking up from all this viewing, they both stated that they were not learning English—they had no use for it. They planned to stay in their homes and eventually return to Afghanistan fairly soon. They claimed they had no desire to understand U.S. culture as the mores and values on television contradicted their religious and cultural beliefs. They had no use, they said, for the United States beyond their husbands working here for a short time to earn money.

Although these women openly denied any benefit this media contact had on their English language development, they were able, with no formal instruction, to discuss characters, plots, and specific events from the soap operas they viewed in English. One of the women even let slip out some lines from television commercials she had memorized.

They were clearly picking up quite a bit of language through television in spite of the medium representing what their religion and culture dictated was taboo.

"Just Entertainment"

A number of interviewees reported (Meskill, 1996) that they felt media was a trivial aspect of their learning and acculturation goals in the United States. Time spent watching television and listening to the radio was time not spent at more serious forms of study. These "studious" folks (some school-age children, some adults) felt that they would benefit more from their time in the U.S. if they engaged more in formal study and less in informal. Media contact did not figure in their notion of what learning English and U.S. culture was all about. To them, media was merely "entertainment."

Interestingly, in the case of a Polish teenager, this view radically changed. Where his initial two years in the United States were dedicated to the schoolwork he saw as being of paramount importance to his linguistic growth, this changed when he became bedridden with a long-term illness. During the months he was sick and in bed he watched television all day. He claimed this had more impact on his linguistic competence than had his more academic endeavors.

Clearly, as teachers we don't want to discourage studiousness. However, listening practice and developing understanding of the patterns of target language interaction remain valuable outcomes of time spent viewing television. As educators, our job is to advocate for a balanced diet of practice. By demonstrating methods for efficient viewing, and highlighting the kinds of learning that result from this form of activity, learners can come to understand alternative ways of making productive use of their leisure time. They can effectively learn ways to practice forms of listening and observing language in action that balances out the full menu of skills language learners need to develop.

IN THE CLASSROOM

Making connections between out-of-class and in-class experiences is critical to effective second language teaching. It is, after all, what goes on daily beyond the threshold of the classroom that truly matters to learners' lives in their new culture. For learners of foreign languages (where the target language is not typically used in the immediate environment), the possibility of target language media contacts grows with publisher, satellite, cable, and Internet offerings. Popular media, being so pervasive in everyday life, is a natural source for making these connections. Students' experiences with television, popular music, and movies comprise motivating material for building a shared knowledge base through which Communication becomes meaningful.

The Media represents a mirror with which learners can examine their native cultures in contrast with the target and, consequently, find a place as an individual within each. Media-related talk and activity can promote critical consciousness of both these worlds.

The Media: Getting to Know Your Students

Assessing the needs, goals, and special qualities and experiences of one's learners is a critical aspect of teaching practice. Careful consideration of learners' media habits and preferences can be part and parcel of this thinking and planning. As mentioned earlier, the topics, characters, and events portrayed in media can serve in making important connections between in-class and out-of-class experiences with the target language. These can be built into curricula and activities that consequently become grounded in student experience with popular media. Understanding learners' media habits can also reveal aspects of students' beliefs and understandings about the world in general, and the target language and culture in particular (recall the Afghani housewives, for example). These can be built upon through in-class activity whereby aspects of media contact are used as either a focal point or as a tool in instruction.

Being knowledgeable about learners' media contact can provide a window for better understanding an individual student's experiences as they relate to the target language and culture. Using media themes, characters, and events as a springboard for student reflection on their own experiences is an excellent method for drawing out feelings and observations of students' lives and learning processes. Understanding learners' relationships with media is critical for teachers in devising and tailoring the kinds of language learning activities that are motivating and engaging and that students will in turn benefit from. Students' habits, preferences for, and reactions to The Media with which they engage can reveal much about personalities and lifestyles as well as how they operate as language learners independent of classwork.

Exploring Students' Media Experiences

The topic of The Media is fertile ground for motivated discourse. Everyone, it seems, has a lot to say about The Media. We hear it, view it, let our thoughts about it foment, and are quite ready to talk about it. The fomenting – the reflection and critical thinking—can be encouraged as part of instructional practice.

Consumers of The Media use their native culture norms and experiences to make sense of what they see and hear. Even in culturally homogenous contexts, one can find learners from varying socioeconomic backgrounds making sense of The Media in startlingly different ways. An extreme example is where a native of U.S. culture would interpret the popular drama *Dallas* in the way the authors, producers, and actors intend, someone from the Middle East might interpret actions and characters based on their cultural beliefs concerning propriety and morality. Indeed, you may find learners from varying socioeconomic and cultural backgrounds making sense of The Media in startlingly different ways than your own.

Take for example U.S. students learning Spanish through a Spanish TV drama. They see a group of eight young people head off to the movies together. In the U.S., the notion of a group of people out for an evening's entertainment assumes that those in the group are paired off into couples. Such is rarely the case in most Spanish-speaking cultures where a mix-gender group of friends is just that. Devising classroom activity that capitalizes on differing interpretations based on personal beliefs and native culture perceptions not only provides an arena for cross-cultural clarification, but optimal opportunity for highly motivated oral/aural practice.

Students' experiences with media can certainly be ascertained in an unstructured, conversational way on an ongoing basis. That is, students can be encouraged to make connections between topics in the classroom and their own recreational encounters with The Media. For example, the knowledge that a number of students watch a particular kind of television show, genre of television show, or favor a particular kind of popular music can be used to promote connections, foster discourse, and expand ideas.

More structured in-class activity might include assigning students to poll one another, others in the learning institution, and/or their families and other people in their communities and, in the case of foreign language learning, speakers of their target language, who either reside in the community or who can be communicated with electronically. Developing questionnaires and interview formats is an activity that promotes a great deal of motivated discourse as it is focused on a very real goal. At the same time it forces a focus on specific language forms and functions (starting and ending a conversation, directing attention, formal versus informal question forms, methods of asking clarification, and the like).

Probing the reasons behind individual media preferences (what this indicates about likes/dislikes, personality) and other reasons for viewing practices (program scheduling, household practices) is an excellent window into the needs, concerns, and habits of students. Students can take responsibility for compiling data on each other and others with whom they have contact. These data can be pooled, observations and implications discussed, and a new shared knowledge base about media habits is in place to be referred to and built upon throughout the language course.

The benefits that can evolve from these kinds of media fact-finding activities are many and rich:

- The Media is often looked to as a vital source of information: information on how to get things done (shopping, cooking, cleaning, etc); information on how those in the target culture behave (this is especially true of children and teens who use The Media to find social norms); and world and local news. Facilitating the use of media for these important purposes can be the goal of classroom activity and out-of-class assignments.

- Students can be guided to reflect on the roles media play in their language learning. Learners can be guided to develop strategies (recalling or repeating a new word or phrase, for example) to further the language acquisition process.

- If students report that in their homes the television or radio is always playing, and if what is playing is or could be in the target language, you can at least be assured that the learner consciously or subconsciously is being exposed to the cadence and intonation patterns of the target language. Likewise, those who are struggling with the sound system can be advised to do the same.

- Understanding learners' media habits can reveal individual interests, priorities, sociocultural attitudes, and even aspects of personality. As such, knowledge of these habits can actually mediate a better understanding of who learners are.

- Knowing the approximate amount of time learners spend engaged with media outside of the classroom can help teachers gauge how that contact might be contributing to the development of their language skills. A student whose behaviors demonstrate little or no skill in a classroom setting, for example, may in fact be spending hours successfully comprehending certain genres of music lyrics or TV dialogue at home.

- As a group, learners can achieve a sense of common experience. Specific characters, plots, and events can be effectively integrated into classroom materials and activities. For example, rather than working with a sentence or passage whose subject is a phantom character named "Tom" as in "Tom used to like oranges, now he likes grapefruit," the name can be replaced by a popular sitcom character's name: "Jerry (Seinfield) used to date X, now he dates Y" or "Homer Simpson used to have hair, now he doesn't" — thus adding a shared, motivating context to an otherwise detached grammar-based language sample.

The incorporation of topics, themes, and specific program offerings into the classroom can encourage students to explore and reflect on how their native and new languages and cultures converge and how they differ. Through activities and processes such as those outlined in Activities A through F at the end of this chapter, learners can develop better understandings of the interstices between their own and the target's cultures, societies, and political systems and how each is represented in media. They can also come to understand the interactions between their first language and culture media literacies and their second.

COMMERCIALISM AND CRITICAL VIEWING

The degree of media's influence on the development of viewers' beliefs, attitudes, and sense of self has been widely documented (see, for example, Fiske, 1987; McLaren, Hammer, Sholle, and Reilly, 1995; Tyner, 1998). The importance of critical media literacy skills is beginning to be recognized in school curricula around the world. Helpful guidelines for parents and teachers abound in training children in selective and critical listening and viewing habits. All this is done based on the belief that children need to be intellectually equipped to see through the guise of entertainment and be cognizant of underlying ideologies. They must recognize the techniques The Media employ to manipulate their emotions and desires and understand that this manipulation is not just part of advertisements, but is woven into the programming around them. For example, it is not by chance that tall, thin women with perfect skin and hair appear in programs interspersed with commercials for diet products, acne medication, and shampoos. Neither is it happenstance that radio commercials for dating services are placed after lonesome love songs.

The purpose of commercial media is to sell products and services. We may sometimes lose sight of this fact when programming and commercials are closely blended. Stepping back and looking at the techniques that advertisers use for the purpose of getting viewers to buy is quite a sobering experience. Not only are our buttons being pushed by the ads, but also, in most cases, the programs themselves are designed to provoke the kind of anxiety that promotes consuming. These programs are then intercut by commercials strategically placed to offer ways to "feel better." In effect, when we listen to the radio or watch TV, our emotions are manipulated for the express purpose of affecting what we purchase. The Media creates a perceived need, then offers products and services to fulfill them.

Exploring with learners how their subjectivities are being shaped by The Media that pervade their lives is an essential task for educators. It is especially critical when viewing a culture other than one's own. As a non-native, the wholesale, unbridled, non-reflective consumption of media risks devaluing one's sense of self even more than it does for those in the native culture depicted. For those from cultures other than what is represented in The Media, they are witnessing material that may starkly underscore that they are *different* from the idealized models of a target or host society they see and hear about. This is potentially harmful to self-image if thoughtful, critical viewing is not explicitly taught.

SUMMARY

The Media transmits sounds and pictures to us for informational and entertainment purposes. In the language classroom, these can be used as tools for understanding and catalysts for meaningful, motivated discourse. Active, critical engagement—the goal of language learning activities in general—can be achieved by incorporating media materials in instruction. Learners can be trained to interact with media in ways that will benefit both their language skills and their identities within the target culture. Moreover, by standing back and gaining a reflective distance on their interactions with The Media, learners can become writers of meaning rather than uncritical readers of others' agendas. They can begin to attend to their own identities as media consumers and how these risk being shaped by the power and pervasiveness of what they consume.

Activities

Activity in the classroom can be tailored so that learners can benefit from exposure to and interaction with the language outside of the classroom. As we saw in Chapter 1, one of the three critical aspects of linguistic growth is attention to Form. Learners can benefit from hearing and interacting with the language if their attention is drawn to its structures and component parts while they are actively engaged in Communication. Media represent an opportunity to not only draw students' attention to the language and cultural components of their texts, but also the structures (metastructures, if you will) or genres of The Media with which they engage. The following suggests ways to incorporate this in classroom work.

Activity A

This activity entails comparing learners' home culture to the target one through media. An off-air recorded clip of the target culture (e.g., students arriving at a high school in the morning) can be viewed without sound. Learners can be called upon to explicate the similarities and differences between what they see in the target culture as compared to their own. This activity accomplishes a number of objectives in terms of language practice (e.g., syntax of comparing and contrasting, common descriptive language). It also trains critical viewing—drawing students' attention to TV images and the powerful messages that images alone carry. Verbalizing similarities and differences also hones interpretation skills in the target language. For younger learners, this is an excellent forum for talking with children about media and culture with an eye toward training critical viewing skills.

Activity B

Just about every community has a local radio and TV station. Those who work as both talent and technicians at these stations make excellent guest speakers. In the second language classroom, contact with native target language speakers who have insight into The Media adds a powerful dimension to a media-using language classroom. The perspectives of media professionals are always a source of interest and insight into our daily contact with radio and television; likewise with foreign language classrooms. It may be more of a challenge to find a native speaker of the language under study, but truly rewarding to learners to bring in such voices from outside the classroom.

Activity C

One activity that takes advantage of the vast repertoire of student knowledge and experience with The Media is writing and producing commercials. Learners from all walks of life understand well the structures and methods of advertising by virtue of extensive exposure. Because of this extensive individual familiarity and because of the motivational quality of advertisements, there is a great deal of positive

Affect associated with an activity involving commercials. This is an excellent form of Communication practice as learners negotiate the selection or creation of a product to advertise, the writing of a script, production, and critique. Focus on Form can easily be incorporated in talk about commercials: the most natural fit is comparatives and superlatives, forms of hyperbole, euphemisms, and imperatives.

Activity D

Just as they are very familiar with the nature and anatomy of commercials, learners are likewise well versed in the genres of TV shows. Genre work in the language classroom can take on any number of variations. As a beginning step, learners can be asked to identify genres and names for them, and adjectives that describe them: e.g., news programming, newscast, newscaster, anchor, segue, top story. Follow up activity might include having learners chart the structures of different genres: how a particular kind of show begins, its progression, plot elements and closure. Comparing structures of the genres makes for motivated discussion that incorporates a range of new media vocabulary and related structures.

Activity E

Weekly viewing schedules can be devised by groups of students who jointly decide on what they will view independently. Groups can then be assigned in-class tasks based on out of class co-viewing. Individuals within a group can be assigned to: 1) sketch a given character in the show to be viewed; 2) construct a key word vocabulary list from the show; 3) make predictions about characters and events in the show; 4) rewrite the ending of the show; 5) compare cultural components to the home culture; and 6) record idiomatic expressions to share with the group/class.

Activity F

The portrayal of women and minorities on television has been the focus of social critique for some time. Learners can be asked to view segments of television and report on the ways in which women are portrayed in the target versus their home cultures. Similarly, the issue of minority representation on television is a powerful catalyst for discussion of race and racism in both the target and home cultures.

NOTES ON INDEPENDENT VIEWING

Conduct a class session on how to use a home VCR as a 'language lab in the living room.' Teach the vocabulary of VCR usage. Encourage students to record their own shows, watch for the gist (sound off), to watch for comprehension (repeat and repeat, study accompanying cues to meaning), and to watch for language functions, gestures, structures, and vocabulary.

Critical 'While-Viewing' Questions to Send Home with Students

Record and watch two to three commercials a few times. Describe what is going on with your eyes closed. Describe what is going on with the sound off.

- Is a problem presented in the commercial?
- If so, how does it get solved?
- What needs and desires are being appealed to?
- Are these needs real, or are they being induced by the commercial?
- Are these needs and desires part of the target culture? your own? both?
- If these feelings are being induced, what techniques are at play?
- Why was this commercial placed the way it was with the show that preceded and proceeded it? Why was it placed in relation to the commercials that came before and after it?
- Will something bad happen if you don't buy this product? What?
- What values (moral, socioeconomic) do the scene and characters in it communicate?

APPLICABILITY

Viewing Guides

Have learners develop a listening guide, viewing guide, and or reading guide designed for newcomers to the target culture. The guide should contain descriptions of local fare (channels, shows, titles), the authors' opinions of these materials for 1) entertainment value; 2) language learning value; 3) cultural value; 4) their adherence to particular ideologies (their ideological/political agenda).

Media Journals

Learners can keep either written or audio recorded journals containing reports of their weekly or monthly media encounters. Some possible specifications for journal entries are:

- use the 'grammar point' or rhetorical form of the week
- connect with experience in the native culture
- connect with a book, an article, or other media encounter in reference to themes, characters, or other chosen focus (which could be a reading from class)
- do a linguistic or cultural explication of an extracted portion (lyrics, dialogue, passage)
- write a critique; what the learner liked, didn't like; agreed with, didn't agree with
- write an alternative ending (rewrite) of the piece
- write a letter recommending (or not) the piece to a classmate or family member

Media Buddy

Pair-up learners for out-of-class, joint media encounters. Have them record their decision-making process regarding what they will listen to, watch, or read together.

3. Principled Uses of Media and Technologies

Learning is a process, not a race.
(bumper sticker)

Chapter 1 traced some key parallels between beliefs that shape language learning and how uses of various media and technology support these beliefs. The pendulum swung between a mediated stance with physical objects and a more "technological" mode of teaching and learning. A tripartite framework for understanding second language teaching and learning was proposed. This chapter examines current beliefs about, and practices in language instruction. It also addresses how these can and do shape the ways media and technologies get used by language professionals as part of their practice. Practical discussion and examples of mediated language learning activities design are included.

COMMUNICATIVE LANGUAGE TEACHING

The past decades have seen a general, widely embraced philosophy concerning the teaching and learning of additional languages. Communicative Language Teaching (CLT) sees communication as the primary locus for the successful acquisition of the forms, functions, and competencies associated with knowing another language well. This stance has emerged from both theoretical and empirical work that tentatively concludes that language learning is optimized when learners engage in active use of the language for a variety of authentic, communicative purposes (e.g., Pica, 1998). The negotiation of meaning with others, in all of its complexity, is generally viewed as central to the learning process.

Communicative Language Teaching – its underlying beliefs, tenets, and concomitant practices – evolved as a direct response to earlier approaches that were strictly form-focused. Such traditional language teaching methods with their focus on discrete linguistic items –principally vocabulary, syntactic structures, and morphology – fell out of favor in the 1960's and 1970's for a number of reasons. Among these was the dearth of linguistic, especially sociolinguistic, meaning incorporated into such practice. Drilling isolated forms devoid of context, it was stridently argued, is not conducive to mastering the intricacies of language as it is truly used in the world. Language learners who received strictly form-focused instruction, it turned out, could conjugate verbs but could not request directions to the restroom in a target language context. Memorization of canned language, bits and pieces of textbook dialogue, and practice sentences did little if nothing to develop one's communicative competence. CLT was consequently born out of advocating for meaning-centered, in lieu of form-focused, instruction: the new belief being that the main route to communicative competence was a great deal of listening and talking in the target language. This is in keeping with the view that mutual negotiation of meaning between speakers activates the cognitive and sociocognitive processes necessary for language acquisition to occur (Breen & Candlin, 1980; Pica & Doughty, 1985; Pica, 1998).

Unfortunately the earliest, and indeed some current practices in CLT reflect a baby-with-the-bathwater approach. In the interest of 'communication,' little or no overt focus on structure can occur. Wholesale, overboard, non-reflective adaptations of these new approaches see learner-centeredness taking precedence over the basic skills and tools required for successful learning. Even though the theoretical genesis of learner-centered approaches emphasize the modeling and instruction of the tools of language and thought which learners would optimally exercise through collaborative, constructivist, cooperative activities, this aspect can get overlooked in actual practice. In part this may be due to the fact that learner-centered approaches require more effort and a more complex role on the part of the instructor. In addition to designing complex tasks and contingencies, learner-centered approaches ideally involve the instructor in systematically modeling and guiding thinking and communication in the target language, activity that is much more demanding than directing learners to have a conversation. Misapplication of CLT-like approaches may be partially the result of teachers:

1. taking the path of less effort and resistance: letting learner 'talk' take precedence over the more demanding work of designing, orchestrating, modeling, facilitating, and undertaking the ongoing, complex work of teaching

2. not thoroughly understanding the increased demands and complexities of their role: not recognizing their role as *choreographers* of learning

In short, balancing instruction to simultaneously encourage the making of meaning (Communication) and focus on Form is not easy.

While not easy, theoretical distance between meaning and form has shortened and the best practices advocated for language education are currently located in a more productive middle ground. That is, the past decade has led us back to considering the value of a focus on linguistic Form tightly tied to active, realistic Communication. This does not reflect a step backward toward the grammar drill days of yore. On the contrary, it brings forms and structures back into the instructional picture in complementary relationship with meaning-based activities. This movement toward an eclectic balance of form and meaning was in part sparked by the diary studies of Schmidt and Frota (1986). While learning Portuguese in Brazil, Schmidt found that when his attention to and awareness of forms were tuned through formal instruction, those structures were then easier to recognize, internalize, and eventually manipulate correctly in those target language contexts he found himself in when outside the classroom. Schmidt developed this notion into what he calls "the noticing hypothesis" whereby the awareness and subsequent detection of form in natural input is a prerequisite for aural or written input to become useful material for the language acquiring mind (see Doughty & Williams, 1998; Schmidt, 1995).

This combined attention to awareness and to meaning makes eminent sense to those who have attempted to learn an additional language. An awareness of the forms one understands and manipulates assists the internalization or "acquisition" of a well-developed linguistic system and a set of competencies that leads to the appropriate application of forms. Having studied another language, you might recall a gestalt moment when a word or structure that you formally studied, that you were made aware of through instruction, occurred in conversation. This *ah-ha* experience—awareness plus meaningful encounter—is central to current CLT + Form focus approaches.

For whatever reason, some might like to portray the direction of this kind of instructional movement as "back to basics." It is hardly that. Rather than a reductionist approach involving the revival of simplistic drills, phonics, and memorization of facts and figures, instructional activity is actually becoming more complex to interweave meaningful, learner-based activities with explicit focus on the tools needed to undertake such activity. Learners thereby successfully gain mastery in both the use of the tools (Forms) and in the effective *use* of those tools (Communication) in contexts and activities that make sense to them (Affect).

Sociocognitive Perspectives

Influential to current CLT beliefs and practice is the broader notion of sociocollaborative learning—a way of thinking about the anatomy of practice and its rationale that is applicable across domains of learning. This *sociocognitive* view of teaching and learning has its roots in the work of Lev Vygotsky, a Soviet psychologist whose work of the 1920s and 30s has had a great impact on current conceptualizations of teaching and learning in the United States and elsewhere. The general theme of Vygotsky's work on learning is the *social* nature of the enterprise. We are social beings who are, from birth, predisposed to learn from the environment, especially from more competent others. It is through active dialogue with these more competent others that our knowledge and skills are built, honed, and later, as fully functioning learned adults, practiced (Vygotsky, 1978). This perspective of learning through social interaction is tightly in line with the foundational aspects of Communicative Language Teaching[2].

Of particular relevance for language learning and teaching is Wood, Bruner and Ross's (1976) notion of scaffolding—mentor discourse that serves to both model and guide an individual's thinking and skills development. Scaffolding is what in language teaching contexts might be referred to as a "linguistic leg up": a question, prompt, or non-verbal cue that assists the learner in understanding and production. In both general and language-learning specific terms, it is this kind of guiding and supportive discourse that constitutes the basic activity of sociocollaborative learning. Given well crafted, authentic tasks with consequences, and guiding discourse (scaffolds), learners develop deeper understandings and skills for making sense of the world. These understandings are grounded in and ultimately manifest in social activity. Such activity can be promoted, motivated, and supported with media and technology.

Constructivism / Constructionism

A similarly useful parallel framework for thinking about roles for objects in teaching and learning is the *constructivism* versus *constructionism* distinction. Construc**tiv**ism is a term that has come to be equated with learner-centered, hands-on, task-based learning. A newer term construc**tion**ism was coined by instructional theorist Seymore Papert (1993). Construc**tion**ism refines the notion of learner-centered discovery and the construction of knowledge to include *construction in consort with others*: construc**tiv**ism emphasizing learner individuality and autonomy in the learning process, while construc**tion**ism marked by meaning-construction *with others* as essential to the process. One need only consider the stark qualitative difference between reading, writing, and

---

[2] Sociocognitive views of teaching and learning also emphasize that *knowledge* as historically defined and sanctioned by a single, restricted sector of the population is invalid. Such views have also fallen under the rubric of 'social critique'; that is, as learner populations become more culturally and ethnically diverse, the act of questioning education's traditional groundings in a sanctioned knowledge base and in singular ways of knowing and understanding the world are suspect. Sociocognitive/sociocultural approaches to teaching and learning value those perspectives that have heretofore been un- or under-represented.

listening practice in a target language undertaken alone as compared to undertaking these tasks in consort with others. The *joint* negotiation and crafting within the constructionist framework more closely aligns with both sociocognitive views and CLT approaches. Negotiation of meaning with others helps second language learners in a number of ways. First, negotiation typically assists learners in comprehending what they hear in the target language. Second, human negotiation is typically characterized by deep engagement. We pay close attention to interlocutors with whom we negotiate meaning. And finally, language learners are forced to produce the target language – something that there is little disagreement about as it benefits the acquisition process.

Language and Culture

As language professionals, it is imperative that we not forget that full understanding of *anything* depends on our ability to perceive the intricate interdependencies between language and culture. In the language classroom this 'understanding' has historically emphasized Big " C " Culture, that is, the great art, literature, and sanctioned historical achievements of the target culture. The role of culture in teaching and learning another language parallels the evolution of postmodern thought. It has, over the last decades, shifted away from the bondage of sanctioned, canonized ways of knowing the world as defined by the powerful and the few, to one that explores, constructs, and validates Little "c" culture, that is, the everyday culture of the masses. Knowledge and understanding of a given culture grows out of study of, and contact with, language as it is used in the quotidian, not in high art and historical/political "achievements." Moreover, this development occurs through redefining self in contact with language and culture *in use*.

A balanced approach to form and meaning retains the best of the humanistic, learner-centered quality of earlier approaches while infusing carefully crafted awareness of the forms, culture, and structures that serve as tools for social thinking, knowing, and communicating. Uses of media and technologies that support such views and approaches are discussed in this and in subsequent chapters.

COMMUNICATIVE LANGUAGE TEACHING, MEDIA, AND TECHNOLOGY

The complementary interplay of sociocognitive, constructionist, and culture-based views and how these are reflected in Communicative

Language Teaching practices can best be understood by reviewing the tenets of CLT:

1. The goal for language learners is communicative competence.
2. Meaning takes precedence over form.
3. Errors are dealt with communicatively
4. Curriculum and activities start with the needs and interests of students.
5. Orientation is toward the integration of the five skills (reading, writing, listening, speaking, and pronunciation).
6. Chunques of discourse are the units of basic practice. Highly contextualized and authentic language is the focus of study.

The following sections discuss each of these tenets and some of the potential roles media and technologies can play in their support. For each of the six tenets, media and technologies are discussed as **models** of target language and culture, as objects of learner **manipulation**, and, finally, as **catalysts** in the teaching and learning process.

Tenet 1: The goal for language learners is communicative competence

Anthropologist Dell Hymes (1972), coiner of the term "communicative competence," defined this term as one's ability to say the right thing, in the right way, at the right time, under the right circumstances, with the desired effect. That is, true mastery of a language is evident when a learner can communicate appropriately and effectively. This broad notion of competence includes a number of interdependent supporting competencies:

- *syntactic competence*: appropriate use (production and understanding) of grammatical forms

- *semantic competence*: appropriate use of lexical items

- *phonological/intonational competence*: production and understanding of the target language sound system

- *sociolinguistic competence*: appropriate use of language to accomplish social purposes

- *cultural competence*: sufficient knowledge of the target culture to accomplish communicative goals appropriately

Models
Media and technology can provide immediate and multiple target language models of communicative competence in action. Such models can provide samples of language use in everyday life from which learners can derive and come to understand the patterns, rules, and norms of target language communicative behaviors.

Manipulation
Unlike direct interaction with the target language and culture, interaction with media and technology is "controllable"; that is, learners can stop and start, freeze, repeat, and study closely the interworkings of language in action. As such, these forms of control and interaction are at once less risky than directly interacting in target language contexts *and*, through instructional routines, attention can be alternated between emphasis on one or more of the component competencies that make up communicative competence.

Catalysts
Media depictions of target language speakers carrying on the business of life in the target culture not only serve as powerful models, and as a resource for observation and manipulation, they can also serve as highly effective catalysts for communicative practice. Tasks and activities that exploit these dimensions of media and technology representations are illustrated throughout this text.

Tenet 2: Meaning takes precedence over form

This CLT principle urges a focus on the meaningfulness of students' utterances and writings. It acknowledges that mistakes in learner production are less important than the messages their utterances attempt to convey and their efforts to negotiate common understanding with others. Primary emphasis on meaning certainly does not eliminate attention to Form; rather, *what* the student is trying to Communicate as a human being with something important to say is heard and responded to before attention is drawn to the Form of what gets written, spoken, or understood.

Models
Media and technology representations (sound, image, and text) can serve as models of the myriad contextual elements that contribute to the making of meaning: listener behaviors and non-verbal behaviors, for example. Video and audio depictions of the messy complex activity of humans communicating can provide much more realistic models than simple text; models from which learners can derive real time strategies for negotiating and getting their meaning across.

Manipulation
When the negotiation of meaning with others is represented in video and audio form, the fact that the words and actions can be stopped, zoomed in on, repeated, skipped, or reflected on can support learner focus on the finer details of communication. In multimedia environments, moreover, learners can not only control the sight and sound of target language representations, but also test themselves on various aspects of the presentation, from simple comprehension to testing the accuracy of their attention to specific forms of negotiation, sociolinguistic strategies, speaker motivations, and the like.

Catalysts
Media and technology can serve as a means for learners to practice attending to broad, gestalt effects of intended meanings conveyed, or "getting the gist," a critical skill when learning a second language. Confidence in both speaking and listening can be built by having learners 'get the gist' of a media presentation and express/defend their interpretations. The richness and density of content, moreover, can serve as a springboard for any number of communicative activities whereby learners talk and write about, through, and with media and technology representations.

Tenet 3: Errors are dealt with communicatively

Traditional views of second language learning saw learner errors as bad habits that had to be broken before they took hold and became permanent. In strictly Form-focused instruction, it is the primary role of the instructor to scrutinize every aspect of student performance and overtly correct these at any expense such as the disruption of communication stream, breakdown of negotiation, negative Affect, and the like. Those who have been students in such classrooms will testify that attempts at using the language become a terrifying proposition; your efforts risk being pounced upon and corrected for the slightest error. The potential for derailment of thought and the possibility of embarrassment are strong.

There are three key reasons CLT promotes the view that errors are not worthy of so much concern:

1. Earlier methods showed overemphasis on Form was made at the expense of meaning;
2. Affect (one's comfort level; overtly corrected errors can lead to discomfort) plays a critical role in learning;
3. Errors are recognized as a sign of learning.

It is now widely accepted that errors are signals that learning is taking place; that learners are successively coming to approximate target sounds, structures, vocabulary use and the like. The position within CLT concerning student errors is that they be treated as part and parcel of the learning process and, consequently, as a natural part of the target language communication stream.

Models
Media and technology can provide models of correct forms. Learners can then compare and adjust their own output. Materials can also supply models of strategies for self-correction, conversational repair, and other productive verbal and non-verbal strategies.

Manipulation
One of the hallmarks of digital technology is that learners can make many attempts by trial and error to achieve correct output. This serves the communicative treatment of errors well. One can make numerous attempts and, in negotiation with the machine and with others, eventually arrive at a correct form. Moreover, in telecommunications environments, learners can review and repair their written communications visually and at a slower pace than in real time talk. Such online talk can also be undertaken in consort with others who may be more capable users of the language.

Catalysts
Media and technologies can record learner output for form-focused review. Audio, video, and text recordings of learner activity can serve as a powerful catalyst for focusing attention on and self correcting errors. In this "after the fact" method, the flow of communication is not impeded by focus on form. That learners are aware of being recorded and that particular forms will be the focus of review can also push them to monitor

their speech and writing more carefully, especially production of those forms that are the focus of a given activity.

Tenet 4: Curriculum and activities start with the needs and interests of students

For language to be used meaningfully, what gets spoken, heard, written, and read must be directly relevant to participants' lives and experiences. In other words, for language to be meaningful, it must be meaningful to those who use it. Communicative curricula are therefore designed for and around learners' needs, backgrounds, and interests. From broad topic selection to on-the-fly examples, choices of language and content are based on who students are and what they bring to the language learning enterprise. In this regard, the relevance and motivation of media and technologies materials cannot be overstated.

The Media and technologies we are most familiar with are designed to be a source of pleasure (e.g., entertainment, valued information, distraction) and, like books, they represent a way for us to further explore ourselves and the human condition. As such, they are highly engaging as well as representative of what learners *need* in the way of language to express their thoughts and concerns. As with any instructional medium, careful choices given the wide range of material can be guided by learner needs and interests and your own good common sense.

Models
What is interesting and relevant to learners motivates their desire to communicate. Models of the kinds of language and the cultural contexts in which language gets used productively are prominent in media and technologies materials. From the language of everyday life represented in popular media (songs, television shows, video games) to the more esoteric or academic (documentaries, content-specific instructional materials, travelogues, educational programming), there are excellent models of language in use.

Manipulation
The added relevance and motivation that learner manipulation of media and technologies brings can ensure learner engagement with material. Selecting, controlling, and changing materials can be orchestrated to maximally exploit interest, relevance, and need as well. Popular video games where there are immediate and interesting consequences are examples of learner-directed activity with immediacy and moment-by-moment relevance for learners.

Catalysts
A good deal of the content of media and technologies represents great springboards for talking about what matters to learners. In a catalytic role, materials can be talked about in many engaging ways that take advantage of what learners know and what they need to know about the language and culture they are studying. As we saw in Chapter 2, determining what is interesting and relevant about materials is also an engaging and productive learning activity.

Tenet 5: Orientation is toward the integration of the five skills (reading, writing, listening, speaking, and pronunciation)

Where once language was considered and taught as a set of separate skills, it is now widely held that skills are interdependent and, as a constellation, form the broadest notion of language competence. The five skills are consequently taught not separately but as skills that naturally arise in tandem with one another when undertaking communicative tasks (e.g., reading and writing for problem-solving discussion). Viewing and listening to, and talking and writing about media and technologies, can be seen as a composite activity complementary to this view. Shifts in focus between the skills in task design and orchestration can be informed by what learners are in most need of practicing and perfecting at a given time.

Models
Media and technologies are packed with models of spoken and written communication. Such models can be used in a myriad of ways to build awareness and reinforce specific skills. They are also ideal as foci for activity that integrates any or all of the five skills.

Manipulation
Most media materials allow learners to shift focus from one linguistic/cultural aspect to another. With audio, for example, attention can be drawn to sound (pronunciation/intonation), the content of what is communicated (comprehension), forms (the structure of clauses and sentences), and to individual vocabulary items. Control and manipulation of representations for these purposes are becoming increasingly common with digital materials.

Catalysts
Media and technology materials are superb catalysts for tasks that involve learners in meaningful practice with integrated skills. Around a small

piece of media, for example, extensive reading, writing, listening, and speaking practice can be designed and sustained. In this case, a segment can serve as a springboard and focal point for any number of integrated skills activities.

Tenet 6: Chunques of discourse are the units of basic practice. Highly contextualized and authentic language is the focus of study

Where the focus of language study was once on discrete, unrelated bits of the target language that were representative of a grammar or vocabulary points, the focus of Communicative Language Teaching approaches is on *language in context*. This means language in all of its complexity and messiness (the language *chunques* you arrive at through chunquing—see next section), not sterile, isolated pieces. Recordings (aural, visual, textual) of target language speakers using the language to negotiate meaning and get things done in the world are now viewed as the optimal authentic material in CLT settings.

Models
Sight, sound, and action are the *sine qua non* of media and current technologies. As such, these multimodal materials can depict language that is visually, aurally, and textually immediate and *in context*. The authenticity of materials—an issue that is taken up with each form of media and technology discussed in this text—obviously varies by genre and purpose.

Manipulation
New media, with links or forms of interactivity of any kind, can be exploited by language learners as a means of accessing contextualized information and relevant links to what they see, hear, or read. In many cases they can also create and/or change what they see, hear, and read in ways relevant to their personal understanding and practice of the target language and culture.

Catalysts
Analysis and discussion of the content and context of authentic media segments is highly engaging and provides important forms for learners to practice speaking and understanding. Media and technology segments can be exploited for their inquiry potential in terms of contexts by having learners probe what they see, hear, and read for new information concerning the target language and culture.

When tasks are carefully constructed to elicit and sustain engaged, constructive student action, the optimal role of the medium or technology is realized; that is, as model, as a tool for manipulation, and as a catalyst for involved, Form-focused, Communicative activity. The following sections suggest ways to harness the power of these tools in practice.

DESIGNING MEDIATED LANGUAGE LEARNING ACTIVITIES: THE CHUNQUING TOOL

Our discussion of designing mediated language learning activities begins with the notion that useful material is comprised of real, not contrived or prescribed language. Historically, language instructors looked to 'the academy' or 'the queen' for a standard of language use for syllabus and materials design. Nowadays, it is the everyday discourse of the masses—how language is *actually used to get things done* by those who are *not* "the queen"—that is the subject of study. Contemporary textbooks have made some progress in moving towards authentic everyday culture and the discourse enacted within it, but it remains the purview of the instructor to continually exercise her discourse analysis skills and abilities in defining the *what to teach* in language teaching.

"Chunquing"[3] is something very experienced language instructors do as a matter of course in their curricula and materials planning. Essentially, it is taking a broad view of language as used in real life target language contexts and selecting elements of that reality that make sense in combination. The resulting "chunque" of language then becomes the targeted material that can be worked in any number of ways to teach the language.

The central question is—given the infinite ways in which language is used in society, what criteria can an activity designer apply to create a tailored chunque for the focus of learning? Traditionally language textbooks perform this function and provide ready-made chunques and accompanying activities. Experienced language instructors are the first to say, however, that this is not sufficient. Textbook materials often need "rechunquing", reanalysis, and expansion to be useful for a given population at a given point in a course. Media and technologies have similar shortcomings in this regard in that they were not specifically designed with your learners in mind.

The **Chunquing Tool** is a template you can use in this task. It can guide you in attending to the anatomy of the language you teach, and in

---

[3] The terms "chunque" and "chunquing" are used here in the context of social, integrative views of language teaching and learning. This spelling is used so as not to be confused with "Chunking", Miller's (1956) cognitive strategy of breaking information into smaller units in order to facilitate memorization and recall.

thinking through, designing, and implementing mediated language learning activity. These suggested processes are by no means linear or simple. They require that a number of considerations be attended to at the same time. Thoughtful construction of language chunques and the design of activities around them essentially boils down to being a good eavesdropper. Listening critically and analytically to the target language as it is used around you is the fundamental basis for chunquing. Being aware of how the target language gets used, employing your linguistic and sociolinguistic competencies in determining appropriacy, and viewing language from the perspective of a non-native speaker—what queries or confusions might that learner have about how the language works—are what make up the chunquing process.

The first thing to understand about this tool is that there is no one right way to go about using it. It can be used to develop, supplement, or enhance your materials in any way you see fit. Because we are dealing with media and technology, we can assume that the Chunquing Tool would be used to either repurpose existing materials (recorded sequences, content-based instructional software, internet sites, etc.) or as a tool to design original materials from scratch (homemade materials). Either way, the place you begin to use this tool to think through your project is completely up to you. Though the skeleton below looks like it should be used linearly, it should not. Start anywhere. Revisit and revise each category as others evolve. Don't stop thinking, adding, deleting, expanding, and contracting until you're happy with the chunque.

Here's what the tool looks like:

The Chunquing Tool

Learners: _____

Topic: _____

Situation: _____

Function(s): _____

Structure(s): _____

Lexis: _____

Skills foci: _____

Cultural notables: _____

Special expressions/idioms: _____

Medium/materials: _____

The chunque: _____

Here's a simple example of a 'from scratch' chunquing process:

You are midway through a 12-week term of teaching integrated skills to low-intermediate learners of ESL. Your three-hour per day course has been an eclectic, integrated combination of reading, writing, and communicative work. Your learners are at a point where they are able to handle fairly sophisticated/abstract topics in their class activities. Their mastery of syntax in their speaking and writing is progressing and they respond well to challenges.

At this point, your low intermediate students have been having difficulty making and responding to polite requests. You've decided they could use some extra practice. You plug in *making polite requests* and *responding to polite requests* under *Function* in the chunquing tool. You then consider the structures inherent in this activity (your eavesdropping and analytic skills are coming in handy now). You write down a couple sample requests from your mental database—***Could you please... I would appreciate it if you... Do you think you might...***—and note that the past modal form is a common and, for your students, challenging structure. You fill in p*ast modals* under the structure heading. But, you realize that *making* this type of request is one thing; you'd better include structures in appropriate ways of *responding*. Again you jot down samples from your internal dataset: ***I'd be happy to, I'm afraid I can't.*** But, wait a minute. Your learners are struggling with the appropriate negative replies to polite requests. You therefore decide to limit *responding to polite requests* to *responding to polite requests in the negative*. This will be sociolinguistically challenging given the complexity of this action in the target culture

Jump to *cultural notables*. Here you note that in the U.S. it is imperative to "soften" a negative response to a request, and that not doing so is perceived as very rude. You jump back up to *structures*: ***I'm afraid I can't. I'd like to but + excuse. I'm terribly sorry, but + excuse.*** Oh, yes, you say to yourself. The excuse. Back down to *cultural notables* where you make a note regarding the absolute requirement of some kind of excuse on the part of a speaker responding in the negative to a request. Back to *structures*. In generating a list of possible responses to requests, you notice that there are apologies of one sort or another built in to each. You also note that if your students are going to practice making excuses, these need to be made a part of your chunque. You add *apologizing* and *making excuses* to the *functions* heading and return to considering the structures inherent in these functions. You note that present modals and "have to" are structures learners will use in politely refusing requests. You add these to the *structures* heading. You need to start limiting the context of these utterances so you begin brainstorming actual situations in which these utterances would naturally occur, and not only occur once, but many times as this will ultimately be the focus of learner activity/practice with this language. You imagine a character who is requesting the unthinkable or the undoable of relative strangers. In what context, in what circumstances might this be authentic? What kind of request would elicit polite refusals accompanied, of course, by an apology? How might the excuse given for refusing be somewhat uniform across those being addressed by the request?

Although there are numerous situations that one can concoct for this linguistic transaction, you choose one you feel confident your students are familiar with, having most likely visited an airport at one time or another, and having followed the news regarding airport security regulations. They have, most likely, been asked by an airline employee, if they have at any time left their bags unattended, and whether someone asked them to put something in their luggage. The *situation* for the chunque, then, tentatively becomes someone in an airport approaching other passengers in the terminal and asking them to watch his/her luggage while s/he runs to the airport's paging phone.

As the situation begins to take shape, you review what you've already filled in regarding functions and structures and see you are on track. Next you start generating a tentative list of vocabulary items that may come into play. You fill these in under *lexis*: e.g., page, guard, luggage, security, terrorism (terrorist, terrorize), prohibited, unsafe. Then you make a list of *special expressions*: against the rules/regulations, catch a plane, running late, ask a favor of, do someone a favor.

You started this chunque with functions, intending for learners to focus primarily on practicing sociolinguistic points, but see opportunities to integrate many more chunque elements as well. You see this as evolving into a chunque that is dense in linguistic, cultural, and sociopolitical issues. You believe that you can get a lot of mileage out of the chunque by integrating skills foci as well by designing multiple activities each with emphasis on a linguistic aspect, skill, or issue. For example, in English when we make a polite request, there is a very formulaic pattern of intonation that looks something like this:

> ExCUSE me (better add that in the function heading—*getting someone's attention*)
>
> Could YOU please watch my LUGgage for a minute while I run to the PAGE phone?
>
> I'm SORry, I CAN't. I HAVE to CATCH my PLANE.
>
> *-or-*
>
> I'm SORry, but it's aGAINST AIRport reguLAtions.

You also note that the structures inherent in this chunque, the present and past modal forms, are structures that your learners would benefit a great deal from reviewing, especially the purposes these structures are put to in such situations. Focus and awareness of these, the functions outlined, and the lexis you've begun to build will serve as the primary focus of the briefs, series of activities, and debriefs for activities related to this chunque. Additionally, each activity will have one or more skills foci, like pronunciation in the case above.

A sample activity generated from this chunque is an extended role play cued by role play cards where one learner is given an A card and his/her partner a B card:

> A: You are running to catch a plane when you're approached by a stranger.
>
> Use: I'm sorry, but …
>   It's against the rules to…

Cues like these can be given to learners as practice using the forms, functions, and lexis in a more controlled communicative activity. More open-ended communicative practice can take place with simple cueing such as:

- A panel of airline customers making recommendations to airline security personnel.
- A scene where an airline check-in employee is told by a passenger that someone indeed handed them something to put in their bag or had offered to watch their bags while they were in the restroom
- A scene where someone is stopped at the metal detector, searched, and nothing is found; or searched and a weapon is found.

Possibilities for extension activities related to this chunque abound:

- going to the international airport security website and researching regulations;
- finding additional sites that discuss international terrorism at airports;
- locating news reports of air bombings;

All can be read, summarized, discussed, and additional expansion activities can be built around them. To integrate writing, students can be asked to write about the situation you've designed or related topics (e.g., letters to airline security officials commending their diligence; accounts to friends or family of their being asked to watch luggage and refusing; recommendations for passengers on how to behave in similar situations). While listening is part and parcel of the communicative activities – learners practice listening to one another during role plays. This can be made purposeful and form-focused. Specific listening activities can be designed by:

- recording a sample/model conversation between native speakers and having learners isolate the forms and functions used;
- responding to a complete-the-dialogue orally or in writing;
- actively viewing airport sequences from film or television to analyze and compare the discourse to that of teacher- and/or class-generated discourse chunques.

A "cultural notable" for a learner of ESL in the U.S. would be that the simple excuse of *I'm sorry, but I'm in a hurry* would be a very common, non-confrontational response. Acceptable responses by country/culture will vary and the issue of these differences is a prime opportunity for discussion whereby students can be chunquers themselves and report on what would work and not work in their native tongue/contexts. Another "cultural notable" for ESL in the U.S. would be the "rush culture"; that is, being in a hurry is characteristic of many North Americans.

Each of the above activities (and these represent just a very few of the many possibilities) requires some fundamental steps to be implemented. The following are suggested steps for implementing mediated language learning activities. The extent to which you choose to employ the chunquing tool is always optional. Remember it is a tool to *think* with when designing and implementing media and technology mediated language learning activities. The following implementation steps, however, are tried and true instructional sequences that serve to focus learners and their learning.

THE CHOREOGRAPHY OF MEDIATED LANGUAGE LEARNING ACTIVITIES

Before
Language learning activities are optimally sandwiched between two critical components: the brief and the debrief. The brief is an essential first phase in the mediated learning activity process. It precedes the actual activity and is opportunity for focus to be drawn to the language, content, and processes of the upcoming activity. At the least this should include the activity's objectives and the proposed means for meeting these. As such, briefing concurrently serves to establish and shape learner involvement in both the processes of the activity and their learning 'stake' in undertaking it.

During
During the actual activity, the instructor engages in close, participatory observation of learner processes using the language, content, and process objectives outlined in the brief as a means of focusing her observations.

She collects data on student action either mentally, through note-taking or by audio or video taping, assigning peer evaluations, or any combination of these methods. Her goal in observing is twofold: to provide moment-to-moment scaffolding, support, and guidance; and to collect material to be used in the debriefing phase of the activity.

After
Debriefing is the essential phase of a learning activity during which the processes (learner behaviors) and outcomes (decisions made, tasks completed) are reviewed and discussed in depth. It is the debrief that affords learners the opportunity to fully reflect on and appreciate what they have accomplished both in terms of the completion of the activity, but also in terms of the language they have used in accomplishing it. It is an excellent personal yardstick for learners to experience a sense of their progress—their second language development. The foci of the debrief are multiple. The process can proceed chronologically or topically with the lead focus of discussion being the language and process objectives put forth during the activity's brief. The instructor guides review and reflection and optimally refrains from offering up any comments that could be construed as judgmental (e.g., *you should have, it would have been better if,* and the like).

Once you have had an opportunity to observe and listen in on students' work (by taking mental notes of strengths and weaknesses in language use) you can use these as the basis for the debrief session. You can point out what students appear to be doing well in terms of the activity's objectives, what they need to work on further, or need clarification on.

The use of a debriefing guide or checklist can help keep the discussion on topic and on target. It is also a written record learners can take with them as tangible evidence of their experience and their learning. Apart from such records, the raw material of the debrief is the instructor's observations about what took place along with those of the participants. Learners' actions, reactions, behaviors, ideas, processes and the language they used make up the material that is typically taken up in the debrief phase of the activity. The debrief can also be used to extend language learning activity by:

- sharing, comparing and compiling task results;
- inquiring about what participants noticed during the activity as regards the language focus;
- noting what got in the way of communication; and
- discussing what learners would like cleared up in terms of target language use issues.

Note that both the brief and debrief represent highly charged opportunities for communicative practice in and of themselves. The debrief represents a rich opportunity for learners to discuss their own thoughts and behaviors in regards to a very immediate, highly invested process. As such, the brief and debrief can typically take up more time, and consequently can be more involved, than the activity itself.

Mediated Language Learning Activity: Roles of the Teacher

Recall that there is a tendency for teachers to interpret CLT as requiring little planning and intervention on their part. Quite the opposite is the case. Form-focused CLT requires the teacher to wear a number of hats, to play a number of very active and proactive roles in its implementation. A language teacher is at once:

-curriculum planner	- discourse analyst	- phonologist	- error analyst	- syntactician
		- conductor		- counselor
-needs analyst	- orchestrator		- facilitator	
		- publisher		- actress / mime
- cross- cultural specialist	- materials developer		- critic	

You may come up with some more by the end of this chapter!

Orchestration / Support
It is ultimately an instructor's responsibility to build a collaborative framework and facilitate and support the activity within it. The instructor designs, implements, and orchestrates processes whereby modes of collaboration are established, sustained, expanded upon, and that serve as fuel for ongoing evaluative purposes. She is, in short, the engineer of productive linguistic activity between and among her students. As such, she relinquishes a good deal of 'teacher authority' in favor of learner expression and independence. The danger with media and technologies, of course, is that that role of authority gets conceptually relocated to the medium or machine. Recall in Chapter 1 that this perception—that the medium or technology carries some agency and authority as a transmitter of learning—is common and to be avoided if your media and technologies use is to be productive.

Media and technology represent authentic opportunities for *cognitive apprenticeship* to take place. In a cognitive apprenticeship, the teacher **models** --in this case the language and behavior to be used and attended to by the students. She **coaches**—gives advice and encouragement as they attempt to approximate modeled language and behavior. And she **fades**—gradually leaves students to undertake task using the language and behaviors she has modeled independently in their collaboration with fellow students (Brown, Collins & Duguid, 1989).

Modeling
The language and behavior that needs to be modeled is, of course, what is authentically required to undertake and fully participate in the task; and, what the teacher has specified as the sociolinguistic objectives of the session.

Coaching
Teacher scaffolding—supplying cues and prompts to give learners the needed 'linguistic leg up'—is very different from mere error correction. Adhering to the CLT tenet that meaning takes precedence over form, the teacher assists learners with composing and understanding messages in ways that encourage communication while attending to the Form of Communication.

Fading
Allowing learners a certain degree of autonomy in their use of the target language, fading logically follows from teacher coaching. The extent to which learners rely on teacher scaffolds and supports ideally diminishes but never disappears.

Media as Material

When instructors facilitate collaborative learning with media and technologies, they count on "the material" in whatever form to help mediate a particular focus and provide tools with which learners can get things done. It is task design that enslaves the material to do her and her students' bidding. Experienced language teachers continually observe the target language environment on the lookout for material and routines that match the needs and interests of students. As with chunquing from scratch, this calls on teachers' knowledge of the target language, the target culture, and her learners. What gets observed and analyzed in The Media can likewise be planned around and incorporated into instructional activity. As a planner and discourse analyst, for example, the experienced teacher has her eyes and ears wide open to language going on around her; the language of everyday life—e.g., casual small talk, formal interviews, asking for something. This eavesdropping and analyzing activity also includes language as it occurs in various media—e.g., the protocol of answering machine messages, radio talk show turn taking, the portrayal of other cultures in film, and the like.

Historically, attempts to capture and offer students the culture of a language under study took the form of foreign language textbook dialogues that were typically used to introduce a structure-based unit of study. Here students were presented a 'slice of life' in the target culture through which they could ideally gain a flavor for how life is lived and how people operate according to their beliefs and customs in the microworld depicted. The not so subtle underlying rationale for the inclusion of these dialogues was and is to demonstrate how the language works in a given context while at the same time introducing new structures and vocabulary that would otherwise simply be a list of words and rules. The intent with textbook dialogues, then, was pedagogical and motivational. The aim was for students of another language to see, in their mind's eye, how language worked in the target land and become involved with speakers' lives, situations, and problems.

Although language textbook dialogues have vastly improved in the past two decades, they still remain fairly sparse in terms of engaging characters, themes, and events. Textbook dialogues do not evoke in their readers the images, empathy, and ethos that a vehicle such as a popular song or a television soap opera does: to feel culture we need to feel the lives of those who operate within it and by its social rules. Those people, then, must have identities, depth, and must operate within situations that allow us to identify with them. Who *is* Señor García? (a character in a dialogue making inquiries about train tickets). What life events are driving him to travel to another part of the country? Can he afford this? What emotions does he experience in doing this? What is awaiting him there?

In contrast to the past where textbook dialogue prevailed, media and technologies allow us to base our models of language in use on oral language and the target culture in addition to texts representing these. Each of the following six chapters treats a different medium or technology: its features, rationale for use, and practical applications. Each type of instructional tool is treated as 'material.' This material can be categorized into three genres: authentic material (pre-existing material that was created for uses other than language teaching); commercially produced material (products manufactured by publishers that are specifically designed for teaching language); and homemade material (teacher/student produced). There are strengths and weaknesses associated which each of these material types. These pros and cons are covered in the following discussion.

Authentic Material

As long as languages have been taught, language instruction has capitalized on all manner of authentic material or *realia* to enhance teaching and learning. Authentic materials can also be thought of as "found" materials. Visuals from the target culture—posters, brochures, postcards, menus, etc.—are standard fare in the classroom. Their authenticity of course lies in the fact that they were not designed for non-native speakers, and as such contain language and culture that is not pared back, sanitized, or artificial. Likewise audio and video material—recordings produced for entertainment and even content instruction—represent opportunities for learners to experience genuine language in all of its authentic complexity. Computer material designed for native speaker use rather than as language instruction is also richly authentic.

Because authentic materials are not authored with non-native speakers in mind, their structure and content have not been tailored in the ways structure and content is tailored in commercially produced language teaching materials. The complexity of the language used has not been simplified. As such, using authentic material represents more investment on the part of the teacher, an investment that can be rewarding for both the teacher and her students who ultimately pick up on this investedness and respond with like enthusiasm. This is in contrast to using manufactured materials that are typically accompanied by a teacher's guide with suggested steps to be followed. While many of these commercially produced guides are quite good and offer clever and pedagogically sound ideas and procedures, they, at least partially, rob both teachers and students of the motivation that comes from having invested in analyzing, brainstorming, and problem-solving one's own ideas and procedures. Examples of the process of repurposing found or authentic media and technology materials will be suggested throughout subsequent chapters.

Commercially Produced Materials

In the past few decades, publishers have increased their language teaching materials offerings almost exponentially. Where forty years ago there were available only plain brown wrapper textbooks, there is now every form of brightly colored, sexily packed manner of consumable imaginable. Where the glitz of commercial products has reached new heights, the basic underlying principle of presenting language tailored to a given level of proficiency remains generally unchanged. The exceptions, of course, are teacher resource or 'springboard books'; texts that provide content, suggestions, and procedures for activities. In this case, the language focus, while sometimes suggested, is the purview of the instructor. Otherwise, textbooks are designed to provide pre-selected, tailored, and consequently, comparatively antiseptic language and content—compared to authentic materials, that is. Again, using a method such as the chunquing tool, one can repurpose commercially produced language learning materials as well.

Homemade Materials

Homemade materials that make use of various media and technologies require a bit of ingenuity and investment of time, but offer large payoffs in terms of student motivation and fit, which is exactly where to begin in conceptualizing the purpose and design of homemade materials.You can use the chunquing tool to write your own news items, articles, websites, record your own audio and video sequences, and exercise your creative talents. The results—homemade materials—make for a more tailored approach to teaching a particular group of learners. Teacher ingenuity in tandem with an understanding of the learners can work to produce materials far superior to commercially produced fare. They are matched to learner interests and experiences; they are an expression of investment on the part of the teacher; they are linguistically and thematically aligned with other curricular considerations; and they represent language in use as you have observed and analyzed.

SUMMARY

There's an old adage in the language teaching profession that goes like this: "Don't change the material, change the method." This more or less translates into, "A good language teacher can teach with a rock and stick if need be." The statement reflects the amount of thought, ingenuity, and talent that goes into really excellent language instruction and that this is indeed what counts, not the 'stuff' you use in and of itself. This chapter has presented some ways to think about the aims and the stuff of the language teaching process – the chunques of language that can serve as a focus of instruction along with a look at what media and technology have to offer for designing, implementing, and supporting the craft.

Activities

1) **Whence Motivation?**

Read the reasons given below. Can you come up with additional sources/reasons for a student's motivation to learn an additional language?

- excitement of engaging tasks, problems, solutions
- collaboration with peers
- competition with peers
- enthusiasm of others (especially the instructor)
- drive to achieve (and satisfaction derived from achievement)

2) All the World (And Especially the Language Classroom) Is a Stage

Like theater, CLT teaching involves planning, vision, and depth of understanding. The teacher can be seen as playwright, producer, director, stage/props manager, audience, and critic. Describe:

- how you see each of these analogous theater roles gets played out in language teaching;
- the qualities you think the language teacher should have to be competent playing each part.

3) With a Partner...

Go back to the six tenets of CLT. With a partner, brainstorm additional implications of media and technologies for each of these tenets.

4) Lights, Camera...

Select a piece from The Media or a computer tool. Script out (chunque) some of the language you would want to hear your students use productively around, through, or about this material.

5) Cue the Good Guys...

Jot down possible cues and procedures you predict would support and sustain the kind of language you've sketched out in activity 2.

6) Taking the Pulse

In her book, *Context and Culture in Language Teaching*, Claire Kramsch (1993) suggests some strategies for scaffolding new notions and the language that accompanies them using what learners already know and have experienced:

- vary the medium or the genre
- vary the point of view
- vary time frame (change periods)
- vary the audience
- vary the referential world
- test out the voices of others

Brainstorm scenarios in which each of these strategies would make sense. Be prepared to state your rationale.

7) Teacher Knowledges

To teach language well, professional language educators need to be versed in a wide range of knowledges – perhaps more than any other discipline. After having brainstormed a language chunque, list out the kinds of knowledges you employed in the process.

4. The Aural: Talking About, Around, & Through Audio Technologies

The ears have walls.
      Anonymous

It's Thursday night. The night before Friday morning's Spanish midterm. For eight weeks Jamie has put off going to the language lab to do her workbook assignments. Today in class, her instructor emphasized the importance of having completed the lab workbook assignments in order to do well on the midterm exam. Jamie is in a bit of a panic. In the first week of class she had tried to sit in the lab, listen to the Spanish tapes, and answer the workbook questions. It had been excruciatingly boring and what was she learning anyway? She understood how to pick out what she thought was the right word or part of a sentence to fill in the workbook answer spaces, but felt clueless as to what these taped voices were really talking about. Nor did she care much. She felt her brain go heavy, eyelids droop, and other matters fill her consciousness. Now she nervously plugs in tape number 1 of 6, opens her workbook and, despite the anxious adrenaline surging through her as she anticipates tomorrow's exam, by exercise number nine, she is fast asleep.

For nearly half a century, since the global embracing and widespread installation of language labs, the majority of language learners have at one time or another struggled like Jamie. The rationale for listening to tapes of native speakers is a matter of common sense, sort of. If one is to learn another language, one must be able to listen to and understand native speakers of that language. Initially, hopes for this technology extended well beyond this 'exposure' rationale. In the 1950's and 60's, the language lab was viewed as a technology that could revolutionize the way languages were learned. The strong association of efficiency with anything technological prevailed, imbuing audio recording and playback equipment with almost magical powers. Given certain frequencies and level of fidelity, languages could be quickly absorbed by up to one hundred learners at a time stationed in their individual booths. The sad truth was and is, however, that only a very small percentage of learners are sufficiently self-directed, motivated, and willing to do, and thereby benefit from, this kind of work.

In some respects this paradigm of individual, autonomous work with technology acting as transmitter rather than mediator persists even today. Recall that the transmission mode of instruction sees the machine as sending information ('learning') into the head of the learner. Language learners continue to be sent to laboratories where, the belief is, the **F**orms of what they hear will get magically (technologically) inserted into their heads.

Fortunately, in recent years publishers of audio materials have attempted to produce more motivating and engaging kinds of recordings and activities to accompany them. Likewise, dedicated language professionals work hard to retrofit laboratory facilities, originally designed for *transmission*, to better suit contemporary practices of teaching and learning. Still, the stigma attached to labs as being boring, tedious, chambers of torture persists.

There are numerous exceptions whereby language instructors have successfully reconceived the audio medium as a venue for active, mediated language learning activity. Here audio is viewed and used as a tool and springboard for constructive interaction—both between learners and between learners and audio texts. In the mediated learning paradigm, audio gets used for active, purposeful listening and invested responding; in short, for meaningful interaction using the target language.

LISTENING

The ears have long been considered the chief perceptual modality for learning language. Hearing language is, after all, the primary way we understand language. But, describing what we do with aural input as simply reception—that is, sounds going into our ears—does not paint a complete picture of understanding spoken language, music, nor even simple noises.

Empirical studies describe a complex interplay of social and cognitive processes humans engage in to understand what they hear. For example, when we listen for understanding, we make active and interactive use of what we know about the world, about the immediate situation, about our own needs and intentions and those of others. All of these elements activate and inform our understanding of the complex streams of sounds we are hearing. In addition, the majority of the learning that we do is informal and experiential. When we learn from aural input, we make use of a vast and complex array of information that contributes to our understanding. This is known as *context*. The denser and richer the context, the more likely we are to be cognitively and affectively engaged. The more we are cognitively and affectively engaged, the more likely we are to fully understand what we hear.

The degree to which we attend to aural input, the amount of cognitive energy we exert, varies a great deal. Very rarely do we find ourselves in situations where we feel compelled to attend to and comprehend each and every word that is uttered. We don't compute and decode every word. Instead we go for the gist of meaning and fill in the blanks with our knowledge of the world and the language being used.

THE ROLE OF THE AURAL IN LANGUAGE TEACHING AND LEARNING

Attention to the centrality of listening for learning and understanding in general, and for learning another language in particular, has only very recently been recognized. Prior to the 1970's, listening was neither an educational concept nor considered a skill that could be explicitly taught and benefited from. If one listened in an instructional setting, this was considered part and parcel of erudite, academic pursuits. It was the words that were sent your way that carried weight, not the act of your interacting with them nor skillfully processing them. Listening was considered to be a passive act of receiving, not doing. Several nearly simultaneous theoretical and empirical breakthroughs have radically altered this conception.

Prior to the 1980s, listening activity in foreign or second language classrooms consisted of *testing* listening comprehension. The thinking went that if students are successfully learning the target language, they should automatically be able to decode the aural version of the structures and vocabulary in their textbooks. Successful decoding typically consisted of supplying the correct response to an objective information question, such as, *What did Pierre buy at the store?* Responses to such questions indicated successful retrieval of bits of information from the aural text. Learners' prior study of textbook-based structures and vocabulary was seen as enabling this retrieval of bits.

Listening is now recognized as an extremely complex activity with full understanding of an aural text entailing multiple forms of cognitive and affective activity. Theoretical work in first and second language acquisition underscores the key role aural input plays in the development of our linguistic systems. Listening has been recast as an activity central to the second language acquisition process (Dunkel, 1991; Krashen, 1985; Rost, 1993), and a skill integral to overall communicative competence (Brown, 1994; Savignon, 1991). Moreover, in some circles listening has also come to be reconceptualized as *the* primary tool for language acquisition (Krashen, 1994). This mutual negotiation of meaning between speakers activates the cognitive and sociocognitive processes necessary for language acquisition to occur (Breen and Candlin, 1980; Pica and Doughty, 1985).

Recognition of listening as complex activity and of its critical role in the language acquisition process has consequently impacted instructional practices. Listening is now construed as an active and interactive process; an activity that enhances learners' listening abilities by putting them in an active role, rather than in one of a passive recipient of aural texts. How does this shift in conceptualization of listening affect how we view listening in the language learning process? Before tackling that question, a little history is in order.

Recall the ways the ancient Romans learned Greek—their second language was first acquired naturalistically, mediated by the immediate environment. Children learned their second language in much the same way as they learned their first, through experiential processes like communicating about their immediate world with others in the home. As with the first language, it was in this way that the sound system, contours, lexicon, and basic structures of Greek became part of their communicative repertoire. With this foundation in place, formal instruction in the language served to draw learners' attention to the formal aspects of the language and to shape competent readers and writers.

This complement of informal, naturalistic processes and formal, technical schooling appears to have combined well in leading to competence in an additional language. The element of *hearing* the target language in its authentic role as it is used to communicate in everyday life, along with the motivation to understand what one hears and to fully participate, are critical components in the overall language acquisition process.

As with learning the native language, initial second language listening activity is a process of growing accustomed to the sound and feel of the language, not decoding complex forms. The sound system itself—e.g., being able to distinguish *cat* from *Kate*—the sound patterns and cadence of sentences—*Wheeeere's the BALL?*—is internalized and a certain low-level meaning is temporarily ascribed. This level of "understanding" requires little conscious effort, a minimum cognitive load. It is an almost somnambulant act much like casually listening to music. One experiences the melodic aspects effortlessly. Where the vast majority of the listening we do entails complex, iterative, and interactive processes, in the early stages of listening to a new, unknown language, listening to distinguish where words begin and end, and/or listening to the overall contours of the sounds comprising the new utterance is unique human activity. This "pre-meaning" listening, it has been argued, is a valued, even an absolute prerequisite to learning the new language.

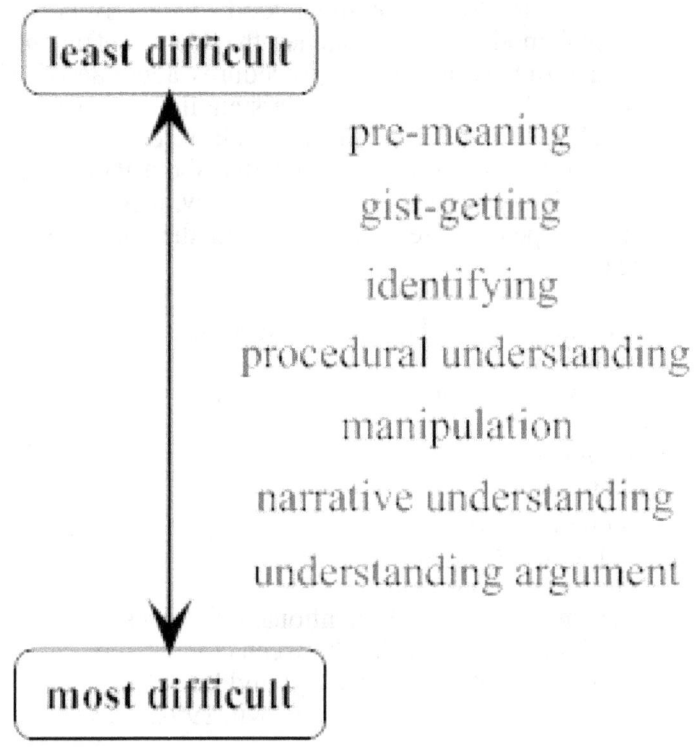

Another level up on a scale of effort and complexity is the activity of *getting the gist* of what one hears. We do this a lot in our native language as a matter of course. We eavesdrop, lend half an ear to the radio or television for the purpose of determining the topic or general sense of what is being spoken. We listen for key words, tone of voice, pace, intonation. From these we conclude a general theme of the discourse.

Not a great deal of effort is expended getting the gist. It is a matter of habit, not skill, and the cognitive load is relatively light as we are going after the general, not the specific. A grade higher in complexity is what Gillian Brown calls *identifying*. This is the act of hearing numbers or terms that are "uncluttered by connotational or associative meaning [and are] identified rather than understood" (G. Brown, 1994:11). This would include PIN numbers, phone numbers, and proper names. Increasing cognitive load by another increment, we get *procedural understanding*. Having a preexisting internal script for a series of actions, we can hear the words that accompany these steps or procedures but, by virtue of our extant schema, do not process these deeply. One simply has to identify the action for which the utterance applies, visualize it, and perform it. For procedures such as diapering a baby, cutting up a squash, loading a computer file, "[to] have understood adequately is to be able to construct a mental model which matches the world sufficiently well to allow you to carry out the necessary procedures adequately" (Ibid.:12). Further up the line of complexity in understanding is what Brown calls *manipulation*. Here the listener must attach referents to names and simultaneously activate background knowledge about their properties and potentialities as well as integrate this with the new, incoming information. In addition, the competent listener can perform the following operations of the utterance:

- elaborate it (e.g., choose more specific vocabulary)
- modify it (e.g., move a phrase within a sentence)
- delete part of it
- add to it
- contradict its content
- paraphrase its content
- summarize its content
- make temporal/causal/intentional inferences based on the relationship between content and aspects of context and background knowledge
(Brown, 1994, p.15)

An even more demanding and complex form of understanding oral input is *narrative understanding*. Add to the complex of activity and options in the previous sections the intricate knowledge of how stories work that we must possess to understand them, and you've got very heavy cognitive demand. However, just we attend to and understand more the faster the aural input, the more closely we attend to, engage, and comprehend stories—at once the most challenging and quite often the most enjoyable of listening pursuits.

Brown caps off her continuum of understanding aural input at the high end of complexity with *understanding argument*. Abstract arguments, explanations, justifications, and theorizing about these are clearly more demanding than other kinds of listening. Following the steps in an argument presupposes a familiarity with distinct forms of Western thought (in the case of the U.S.) and modern, scientific reasoning, abstract terms and their interrelationships, and a myriad of additional complex and demanding forms of cognition. Quite a bit of higher-level classroom activity consists of this kind of listening.

The Audio Medium

As one listens, hypotheses are formed, tested, modified, accepted, and rejected. Perhaps the most compelling feature of audio technology in this regard is the fact that recorded audio can be manipulated to support such purposes. Portions of the aural stream can be isolated, skipped over, edited, replayed *ad naseum*, amplified, and, if you're into *Sergeant Pepper's Lonely Heart's Club Band*, reversed entirely. Cryptic messages aside, these capabilities can be used as powerful tools to aid the listening and understanding of spoken language, especially a new one.

The audio cassette tape is still a relatively convenient, inexpensive, and flexible medium for creating and playing back sound. Like all other forms of information, this form of analog technology has largely been replaced by more versatile digital technologies. Even though an inexpensive cassette + CD stereo is all you may need to record, edit, and playback audio in your instructional activities, digital audio in the form of .mp3, .wav, .rm, all forms of digitally encoded sound have become both inexpensive and ubiquitous. Portable media players, also capable of storing and playing back audio files, are equally available and inexpensive. Digital recorders allow teachers to capture authentic conversation.

Digital recording and editing have tremendous advantages in terms of precision, access, and storage. For editing purposes, you can isolate segments to the millisecond and recombine these any way you wish. Almost all recordings made today use some form of digital editing and multitrack recording for these reasons. The cost of newer recording/mixing/editing devices and computer software that facilitates these processes has fallen well within the range of most school budgets and will continue to fall as new advances are made in digital technology. There are numerous resources on the Web that can now assist you in making customized recordings.

It is possible to store literally thousands of hours of music and audio segments to be played back on a computer. The ability for teachers to find almost limitless amounts of sound files on the Internet means that the language classroom can be transformed into an environment where authentic target language can be heard at any given time. All that is needed is a computer or digital music player and a set of speakers. Regardless of the content area, audio segments can help stimulate any number of powerful instructional events. From simple sounds in daily life (identify, solve a puzzle, determine mathematics of rhythmic structures, re-edit to make sense of procedures used in a scientific experiment, etc.) to recordings of voices from the present (a National Public Radio piece, a Supreme Court hearing, popular musical groups) or 'voices' of the past (Poe, Darwin, Abzug), learners can be guided to attend to, react to, and control the content of audio segments to great advantage.

Audio as 'Material'

Below is a list of some suggested roles that audio materials can play in mediated language teaching and learning activities. It is presented as a starting point in conceptualizing audio as material beyond simply a source of sound.

Information Resource
Recorded audio sequences can be used as sources of information. Tasks requiring purposeful listening, the extraction of information that is necessary to complete a larger task, the sharing and presentation of that information, and collaborative processes around fitting that information into a larger picture to solve a problem constitute powerful acquisition-oriented processes. The active learning does not stop once the learner extracts information from an audio source; she then goes on to make use of that information in a larger task with others. The information and the act of getting it then carries a sense of purpose and investment.

EXAMPLE: **The Murder Mystery Chain**. Record or use prerecorded clues to solve a murder. Have learners move from recording to recording, extracting the information they believe they need to solve the crime. They can work as individual "detectives" or as teams. Provide language chunques that match the task and learners' level for them to use in compiling and negotiating a solution.

Modeling
Audio materials are extremely useful in modeling native speaker discourse. Not only does recorded material bring in new voices apart from the teacher's; it is also controllable and manipulable. Learners can therefore start, stop, rewind and repeat to study closely the structures, subtleties, and nuances of native speaker discourse. The focus of the recorded model can be multiple: learners can zoom in on particular sounds, patterns of intonation, expressions, functions, structures, or vocabulary. The degree to which they attempt to imitate these is dependent on their current needs and level of ability. For learners whose native language patterns of intonation differ radically from those of the target language, recorded models are an excellent source of practice for them to hear the target patterns and attempt to imitate these. Audio recordings can also serve as models for learners to refer to in scripting and making their own recordings. Learners can work to imitate the format and discourse patterns of the radio talk show, news show, or variety show.

EXAMPLE: Record brief segments of a target language soap opera. Assign individual learners to study specific characters in the scene (personality, past, melodramatic technique, and discourse style). Based on these models, have learners extend the action in the recorded video into improvisations by their assigned characters.

Stimulus for the Senses
Many a language instructor has discovered the value of recorded sounds or music as a tool for 'setting the scene' for a language activity. Music, a series of sounds (natural or artificial), and even poetry are excellent material for establishing a particular mood and provoking learners to think or imagine in advance of a related activity: writing, discussion of a topic related to the recording, pre-reading schema setting, listening to related dialogue. In a language teaching method known as *Suggestopeadia*, baroque music is played in the background while the instructor reads a story aloud in the target language. When done well, the reading's cadences match up with those of the music to produce what the method's developer, Lozanov (1978), terms "Super Learning." I have heard teachers report on their use of baroque and other types of soft music as background to all sorts of language learning activities. They see it as having both a calming and focusing effect on learners. The aspect of focusing is an important one in language learning and one you may want to consider as part of your audio-based planning.

EXAMPLE: Record a brief piece of music that sets the scene for your current theme or topic; for example, if you are studying the language of travel, record a piece of music that reflects movement and travel from the target culture. This recording can be played as a way to set the scene, as a stimulus for introducing or expanding on the topic, or as an assignment in brainstorming whereby learners listen and jot down their impressions using target language vocabulary.

Springboard
Just about any kind of audio recording can be utilized as a springboard for language learning activities. Some that work particularly well are recordings that concern controversial issues, present problems in need of solution, and dramatic scenes subject to multiple interpretations. Such 'springboard' material can serve as a stimulus for talk and activity.

EXAMPLE: Record a brief segment from a news program from the target culture. Set the scene by discussing the topic addressed in advance of learners listening to the segment. Have learners listen with the intent of taking a stand on the issue in a post-listening discussion.

Information Gap
Information gap activities are popular, highly motivating language learning exercises. They induce active, invested negotiation of missing information and as such make for excellent practice in the target language. The principle for their design is simple: information is provided

to an individual or group; different information is supplied another individual or group—the two factions must find out the other's information to reach a conclusion, solve a problem, or complete another kind of task. Audio materials can serve several purposes in an information gap. They can be used to set up the activity by supplying: 1) information to all participants; 2) information to those who need to fit it with information supplied to others; and, 3) information to the logistics for undertaking the task.

Playing a recording of 'the problem' (e.g., hearing a conversation that reveals a dilemma) is a solid means of introducing an information gap activity. The recording can also spell out directions learners will need to follow to undertake their assignment. Having different individuals or groups privy to different pieces of recorded information is one way of making good use of recorded materials; again, learners will be highly invested in the listening process so they can be equipped to negotiate and be successful at the task.

EXAMPLE: Record monologues by family members who are concerned about the love life of someone in the family. Assign individual or small groups of learners to listen to a specific monologue. Each monologue reveals a piece of information about the love life of the focal family member. Learners have to then use the information they have in consort with the information of other class members through their assigned monologues. The goal is to merge their pieces of information to make recommendations for the focal family member to proceed with his/her love life.

Brain Theatre
"..language does not describe a pre-existing world, but creates the world about which it speaks" (Winograd & Flores, 1988, p.179). Learners come to the language learning endeavor equipped with imaginations. Stimulating those imaginations while practicing the target language can be achieved in any number of ways. Audio recordings of dramatic scenes, series of sounds, and certain types of music, for example, can be used for something I call *Brain Theatre*. Learners listen and attempt to describe their visual experience of the aural material. They can be prompted with visualization questions such as, *What color is the carpet in the room,? What is X wearing on her neck?* The language that learners generate then represents their own personal vision of what was aurally stimulated. Brain Theatre can be used to "set the scene" for an activity, or as an activity in and of itself.

EXAMPLE: Record a series of simple sounds (e.g., a car horn followed by a cat meowing, followed by a heavy object falling, etc). Have learners listen with their eyes closed and compose a story about what they hear. Stories will vary a great deal and be a rich source for comparison and discussion. Chunquing the stories on the fly will also help provide focus on select vocabulary items and syntactic forms.

Illustration
Audio recordings can be used to illustrate dialectal differences in the target language (regional accents), the discourse habits of individuals with specific personality types (hyper, arrogant, shy), or the ways in which speakers of the target language may respond in given situations (knee-jerk reactions from those of particular political persuasions, a fan at a sporting event, a teenager's self-righteous indignation). Using audio recordings for illustration differs from using them for modeling in that the purpose is not for learners to imitate what they hear, but to increase their range of understanding.

    EXAMPLE: Record from radio, TV, or Internet clips a sampling of different target language dialects. These samples can be played as part of a discussion of target culture geography, a current event, a piece of literature, or in the context of pronunciation work.

Cloze
Focusing learners' attention on specific forms, functions, sounds, or lexical items within an audio passage is nicely done with the accompanying text of the audio sequence. Those items to which you want to draw attention are deleted. Learners can listen repeatedly to songs, monologues, dialogues, commercials and the like to fill in the blanks you have inserted into the text.

    EXAMPLE: Record a popular target language song that contains many verbs in the past tense. Transcribe the lyrics while deleting the past tense verbs. Have learners listen to the song (and sing along if they wish) and fill in the missing verbs.

One-Sided Dialogues
One-sided dialogues are fun, challenging, and easily recorded. Here's a beginner level example:

    A: _____
    B: Hello. I'd like to speak to Mr. Gershwin, please.
    A:_____
    B: Oh, okay. Never mind. I'll call back another time.
    A:_____
    B: I said I'd call back later.
    A:_____
    B: Yes, that'll be fine. Right. Goodbye.

Dictations
Alternatives to straight dictation exercises include designating groups to listen and transcribe every other line of a dialogue, song, poem, or passage. The groups then put their lines together into a coherent whole. The very simple nursery rhyme, *Solomon Grundy*, is one example of learners reassembling what they hear and transcribe:

>Solomon Grundy (Group A)
>Born on Monday, (Group B)
>Christened on Tuesday, (Group A)
>Married on Wednesday, (Group C)
>Took ill on Thursday, (Group B)
>Worse on Friday, (Group A)
>Died on Saturday, (Group C)
>Buried on Sunday: (Group B)
>This is the end (Group C)
>Of Solomon Grundy. (All)

Student-Made Recordings
Students, like teachers, are hams. Not only that, they generally enjoy (or are learning to enjoy) hearing themselves as speakers of another language. There are many activities that involve learners listening to one another's recordings. These can be reviews, critiques, poetry readings, commercials, personal musings, the presentation of personal dilemmas—real or fictional—for which other students record a response.

Students are also good at making original cloze exercises for one another. They choose the passage, transcribe it, delete the focal items, and have classmates complete them. They can also collaboratively design and record their own puzzles and problems for classmates to solve.

AUTHENTIC VS. REPURPOSED VS. COMMERCIALLY PRODUCED AUDIO MATERIALS

A note on commercially available recordings: when making decisions as to whether to use commercially available audio recordings, — recordings designed specifically for learning language—be aware that there are many more types and genres now on the market in addition to traditional workbook drills. Authors and publishers have "gotten religion" in terms of producing more authentic sounding audio around which come packaged motivated, communicative tasks. In many cases publishers offer demonstration/review copies by mail or allow you to sample their recordings via their web pages (see Appendix). It is certainly worth reviewing these samples for ideas for your own productions and repurposings; and for possible purchase and use. Commercial recordings may be a worthwhile investment when they are technically superior, and will save you the work of undertaking the kind of extensive content analysis (chunquing) required when making your own or using existing recordings.

Homemade Audio

Teachers are born thespians and homemade recordings are a great outlet. Your tailored recordings can personalize materials to include students' names and details that relate directly to their lives (places, events, issues). In preparing to record materials, you need to consider where you wish the end product to lie on the continuum of scripted-spontaneous recording.

If your aim is authenticity, tightly scripted material is more challenging. Through the act of writing out the exact utterances to be spoken, much of the authenticity of spontaneous speech is lost. There are many instances, however, where tight scripting is desirable: for example, recording a simulated lecture, a theatrical reading, or a radio commercial.

In the center of the continuum lies the semi-scripted approach. Here you go so far as to jot down key words, expressions, and forms you wish to be the focus of attention and a rough outline of how the conversation begins, develops, and ends.

For a purely spontaneous recording, try this. Three minutes before class, invite a target-language speaking colleague to chat about anything—a mundane event, current news, simple social exchange in the language you are about to teach. The end result will be spontaneous and, because it is human communication, most likely fairly messy. This one minute (or less depending on the level of your students) segment can be used in class for a range of engaging and authentic listening and speaking activity; for example, learners can be directed to listen 'for the gist' one time through and discuss/debate what they gleaned. They can also be directed during a second or third playing of the tape to note new words, forms, or expressions. A brief spontaneous piece such as this is also a good stimulus for Brain Theatre (see above). This kind of brief encounter with spontaneous native speaker speech where learners achieve some level of comprehension is a valuable confidence builder and provides excellent holistic and discriminatory listening practice.

Tailoring audio recordings can serve the particular learning needs of a given group (e.g., Arabic recognition problems with [b] [p]). Audio recordings can also be tailored to topics relevant and germane to a given group: for example, middle-aged adults who will soon be responsible for taking care of their parents in their old age can listen to target language speakers discuss the same issue.

Audio scripts can also play around with reality and use humor to motivate listening. For example, students love to pick out mistakes, so plant some in the script: e.g., *I just got back from buying vegetables at the post office.* Such bloopers can also activate the imagination in unique ways. Additionally, sounds, music, and tales can be used to provoke learners to describe and embellish the images they evoke.

Repurposing

Recordings originally produced for native speakers of the target language are often motivating (e.g., songs, dramatic readings) and, with some re-engineering through chunquing, they can be used very effectively as language teaching material. Again, recordings made with native speakers in mind is an excellent way to bring new voices into the classroom and/or laboratory.

One extension activity suggested by Earl Stevick (1976) is the use of imagery questions. Similar to Brain Theatre, these can be used with any type of recording with varied purposes. The overall motive for including imagery questions is to bring immediacy and meaning scaffolds to the listening process by asking learners to activate their visual imaginations while listening to a passage. Below is a very simple example. Keep in mind that imagery questions can be asked of any recorded piece.

Learners hear:
Sue: Oh, it's time for me to get going.
Lou: That's too bad. I hope we can get together again soon.
Sue: Me, too. See you.
Lou: Yeah, see you.

Sample Imagery Questions:
What is Sue wearing?
Where are they speaking?
What color are the walls?
What time of day is it? How is the light?
Describe the expression on Lou's face.

In sum, advantages of using repurposed or homemade tapes include:

- gets new voices into the classroom
- intrinsically more motivating to listen to real rather than 'clinical' speakers
- more representative of what happens when language is used to communicate (less scripted)
- reflects the critical factor of contextually determined meaning (not made in studios)
- representative of what learners will hear in the target language community (more authentic than studio productions)

AUDIO LABS: BEYOND THE BOOTH

> *...already within the profession there has grown an unfortunate cleavage between "book men" and "lab men"*
>
> (K. Mildenberger, on language laboratories, U.S. Office of Education, 1962)

A present day audio laboratory is not just that. Traditionally, this is a facility that provides individual audio stations at which students can work independently, in groups, or as a whole class. They became very popular in the 1960s due to the growing trust around the world in things technological, especially when applied to "problems" in education such as the failure of foreign language instruction in the United States. Nowadays, the majority of language laboratories offer more than just audio recordings.

Independent work in an Audio Lab

Some of the self-study options in an Audio Lab include:

- listening dictation (listening to a recording then transcribing what one hears)
- drills (hearing then repeating what one hears)
- note taking (listening to a recording and writing down key points)
- comprehension practice (listening to a recording and responding to comprehension questions)

- listening for pleasure (listening to recorded music, stories, or other entertainment genres)

Undertaking 'independent' work with audio works well for a small minority of language learners who are sufficiently self-motivated and who possess the skills and strategies to engage in self-directed study. Ideally, self-study activity would include doing a great deal of 'noticing' of linguistic forms and sociolinguistic functions. To maximize the effects of independent work it is also desirable for learners to exercise good learning strategies in dealing with comprehension and content. For students who are less motivated and well-equipped for this kind of activity, two tactics may be in order:

1) Training in learning how to learn
A brief session reviewing some of the simple strategies good language learners use with the audio medium may provide a "leg up" to learners who are less well versed in employing good strategies. A simple checklist and some examples, such as these below can remind and focus learner effort:

- Clear the decks: remember the Mozart studies. A deep breath, a moment's clearing the head will improve your ability to concentrate.
- Jot things down. As much as you think you'll remember a word or expression, you probably won't unless you write it down.
- Use imagery. Place what you're listening to in a visual context of your own creation.
- If you're viewing video, use the visual to make good guesses about what you hear.
- Repeat, repeat, repeat. That's what that button's for.

2) Invested Work
Another tactic is to create a sense of learner investment in independent work. This requires designing audio-based tasks that learners undertake independently but for which there is some form of meaningful accountability to others in the class. The work a student does alone with audio materials, in other words, carries some consequence in the larger goal/task of others. One example would be to have individual learners 'research' a particular audio text—a mystery, for example—to extract clues about a specific individual, location, or time period. Built in to this task—if it were thoroughly chunqued—could be work with a particular set of forms, functions, and lexis. The learner works individually, with a specific task guiding interaction with the medium, then brings back the

assigned material and any thoughts and observations about them to be considered and incorporated by the group as a whole.

Once good aural learning strategies are understood and practiced, there are any number of tasks that can be designed and assigned individual learners with audio texts. These can be viewed as belonging to three broad (often overlapping) categories:

1) Achieving Understanding
2) Extracting
3) Responding

Under the first category, *Achieving Understanding,* learners can be assigned to make sense of audio text passages (one or a series of passages) and bring back to the class an articulation of that understanding. *Extracting*, as exemplified in the mystery example above, can be assigned to any sort of audio text. The critical component is that the information extracted must feed into a larger task where the information obtained by one student interfaces with other pieces retrieved by other students. The extracts can act as a source for discussion, for solving a problem, or for creating new problems and questions for learners to tackle. *Responding* to aural texts can consist of learners listening to passages and recording orally or in writing their reactions and responses to the passages. This works particularly well with drama, poetry, works of fiction, and dialogues on contemporary controversial topics of interest. In any case, the 'individualized' listening experience becomes one that is charged with individual accountability and investment as what the learner does with the audio material is brought back to the context of the classroom community and thereby valued.

Group Activities

Some pair, small group, or whole class activities in an Audio Lab include:

- role plays (these can be recorded and played back)
- extended simulations (learners take on roles and record their 'parts' in the simulation)
- performances (songs, dramatic readings, etc. can be recorded for presentation)
- problem solving (learners rotate between recorded clues/information to solve a problem—"information gap")

- discussion (recordings listened to by pairs/groups/class can serve as springboard for discussion).

Grouping learners for work in an audio lab works as well as the design and orchestration of tasks learners undertake. Setting up group work in a language lab differs from doing so in the classroom in terms of physical logistics, materials, and the fact that there are machines to deal with. Recorded materials must be prepared and access to them arranged in advance. Machines must be checked to assure they are in proper working order, and hardcopy materials prepared.

The Anatomy of Audio-based Listening Activities

The key to designing successful audio-based activities is to remember that the task is everything. The materials themselves don't matter a great deal; remember, we listen to all sorts of flotsam and jetsam in our daily lives and have developed skills accordingly. These are important skills developed through listening to what has not been pre-selected nor tailored to our perceived abilities. Language teachers *can* tailor *tasks,* however. The same listening materials can be used in classes with a range of proficiency levels if the task is tailored to learners' abilities. An authentic, fast-paced native speaker conversation, for example, can be used with beginning level students who are asked to simply 'get the gist', with intermediate level students who are asked to focus on one or more designated language structures or functions, and with advanced learners who take on the roles of particular speakers to alter or complete the conversation. A list of sample tasks follows.

- *Pre-listening warm up (schema setting)*
  This can be accomplished by showing a picture that sets the scene, writing a word or two on the board, or asking probing questions.

- *Language focus made explicit*
  Letting learners know what they will learn is a fundamental aspect of any instructional activity. Writing the focal form, function, and vocabulary items on the board or on a handout alerts students to what they should focus their attention.

- *Assign tasks while-listening*
  Learners should always listen for a purpose. Ideally they should be *physically* doing something while they listen. For example, if they are listening to a passage that entails locations and/or movements, having them follow on a simple map or layout as

they listen cues their listening focus and gives immediate purpose for their listening efforts.

- *Reactive listening*
  Purposeful listening, task-based listening, means that learners will have something to say, something to contribute once they have listened and accomplished their assigned while-listening task. Provide the forum for their reactions and contributions.

- *Debrief and assessment*
  Learner sharing of their listening experience (be it in the form of information extracted, personal reactions or opinions stimulated, etc.) can serve as a learning assessment. How well learners understood the recording, the task, and the focal language point(s) can be taken up during the listening debrief.

- *Post-listening task*
  It is useful to build-in an extension activity whereby learners make use of the themes and language of the recorded piece. If learners followed a speaker from location to location on a map, for example, a post-listening activity may be for them to write up the series of movements from place to place into a story of their own making.

AUDIO: BEYOND THE CLASSROOM

Truly self-directed language learners may make use of analogue and digital audio devices to practice listening and speaking on their own. The benefits for ongoing practice once outside the classroom doorway cannot, of course, be overstated. We would like all learners of another language to have contact with it every waking hour, indeed to dream in that language! It is worthwhile discussing this option for additional practice with learners who may not otherwise see the value, or lack the impetus to use recordings outside of class. You may even want to assign the long-term project of having students keep a record of their out-of-class listening throughout the term. Such an assignment can be facilitated by making easy listening, entertainment, music recordings available to students to use in their spare time; and by asking learners to keep a log of:

- new structures they hear

- new vocabulary
- cultural queries and notables
- issues of linguistic pragmatics

Fluency Journals

An excellent use of the audio medium is to have students maintain fluency journals. These consist of daily, weekly, monthly, recorded entries to which the instructor, peers, or native speakers you can recruit from the community respond. Like written journal responses, recorded responses can focus on both Form and meaning, thus giving the learner practice in speaking, listening, and form-focused review.

Pronunciation Work

It is not unusual for learners to have difficulties with particular aspects of target language pronunciation and it makes good sense to have them work with individually tailored recorded materials to help them hear and imitate problematic target sounds. Once you've assessed the areas of difficulty an individual learner has, you can record models for her to listen to and imitate outside of class time.

Songs and Memory

Many language learners report memorizing the words to songs and movies in the target language. This, they report, helped them achieve a "feel" for the language even though in many cases they did not fully understand the words and sentences they had committed to memory. Using familiar songs as a focus for Form and meaning-based work is an effective and enjoyable teaching strategy.

SUMMARY

This chapter has presented a case for using audio technologies as mediators of language learning. Praise for the medium in the traditional sense of its providing rich representations of native speakers in action, as a means for learners to exert control over the pace and presentation of the target language, and as a critical tool in achieving target language competence, remains valid. Audio represents a rich source of linguistic and cultural material when it involves learners actively in making sense of the target language for specific, sociocollaborative purposes. As such, audio is a powerful tool for acquisition-oriented instructional activity. The medium can serve as a resource, springboard, and tool for communicative purposes. Learners can talk about, through, and around it. Learner-centered, mediated notions of teaching and learning can extend and enhance this medium that has historically made good pedagogical sense as an instructional tool.

Activities

A Matter of Character...

Listen to a brief selection from a commercially produced recording designed for language teaching. Select one character heard in the selection. Write a letter to this person. Is s/he easy to imagine? Do you have a sense of that person's history and identity? How much effort did you expend inventing this person's character?

For a Short Time Only...

Record a brief series of radio commercials in the target language. State their genres and the conventions they use. How are these effective?

5. The Visual: The *Why and How*

...no representation can fully exhaust the images, feelings, and meanings emergent from an event.
(E. Bruner, 1983:6)

In this chapter, the term *visual* applies to pictures, film, television, videos in both analog and digital form. These are all readily accessible and inexpensive media that, when thoughtfully used, can add important dimensions and play powerful roles in the language classroom. We begin with a look at *why* using visuals in language teaching and learning can be additive and productive. Samples of various pedagogically-grounded uses (the *how*) follow.

The *Seeing* Metaphor

In English, the seeing metaphor pervades our daily language and, argues Lakoff and Johnson (1980), in many ways shapes our perceptions. As users of language we borrow from the physical and social world to generate meaning for less accessible notions that are related to mind and emotion. We take what we can readily know and understand through our concrete, physical reality and apply these to the more abstract things to which we need to refer and use in the language we speak. This notion of moving from the physical to the abstract is richly evident in the pervasive metaphor – *seeing is understanding*. Before we examine how this metaphor works in our production and comprehension of language, a story:

> When an early explorer asked the Australian aborigine what the name was for the strange creature they saw on landing on that continent, the aborigine answered "Kangor-oo" which means "I don't know" in the aboriginal Australian language.

How is it that we know when someone points to a dog and says "dog" that they are not referring to the tail, its breath of something it just did? We have uncanny ability to figure this out. We can read the intention of the speaker and know that the intention is 'label the dog' rather than explain a sudden odor. If the speaker's intention was indeed to explain the origin of the sudden odor, as competence communicators, we would immediately infer this through subtle contextual clues indicating the speaker's intention. In the kangaroo example above, the communication was unsuccessful because the intention of the speaker was not clear in relation to the thing seen (the kangaroo).

Visuals occupy a significant space in our experience of the world around us. Our vision is our primary means of knowing our physical environment. It also involves a good deal of processing as in picking out objects from their background or to differentiate features, for example. What is particularly important to language instruction is the fact the seeing is a similar experience for people who have the same vantage point and can thus talk about what they see as *shared knowledge*. Think about a class of language learners who simultaneously refer to a visual using the target language as one such instance of this of this shared knowledge.

Returning to the *seeing as understanding* metaphor and its centrality both in our every speech and perceptions but also in language education writ large, have a look (pun intended) at the following language:

> I *see* what you mean.
> The argument *looks* different from my *point of view*.
> What's your *outlook* on the project?
> Let me *point out* a flaw here.
> OK, I've *got the picture*.
> Your *point* is very *clear*.

Indeed, the verb *to see* is from the Latin *sequor* meaning to *follow*, another metaphor the physical movement for which aligns with our understanding of a sequence.

One way we use visuals in language education is in a middle position with the teacher orchestrating communication around this shared point of focus. She uses and elicits target language that is represented in or can be related to what is commonly seen. Other formats for including visuals in the instructional conversation include pairs taking with, through and around still or moving images, students and even the teacher talking spontaneously about what is in the visual and beyond, making associations between what is seen and other points of common knowledge and understanding, and, of course, as a reminder/point of reference for target language vocabulary and/or target language cultural information. In each case, the visual serves as a force in communicating authentically for the purpose of mastering aspects of the target language determined by the teacher by design (Chapter 3).

VISUAL COMPETENCE: A COMMUNICATIVE COMPETENCY

Laurence Wylie (1985) made the claim that 90% of what gets communicated in face-to-face conversation happens visually; not through language, but through non-verbal communication, meaning the body, the context, and extralinguistic noises. Indeed, the field of socioevolutionary biology confirms that the human sensory system is geared to process mostly audiovisual information (Cosmides & Tooby, 1992). This is best reflected in the amount of vocabulary in human language related to audiovisual processing. Anywhere between a whopping two-thirds and three-quarters of any language is comprised of words that refer to hearing and vision (Johnson, 1987). This predisposition is also reflected in the behavior of newborns who very quickly fixate on faces, facial expressions, and familial voices as precursors to the development of communication skills (Boysson-Bardies, 1999).

Simply watching two characters talking to one another in a video or on TV with no sound and being able to understand the flavor, if not the fine particulars, of what these characters are saying, is proof positive of Wylie's notion. The process of learning another language can benefit a great deal from both an awareness of the amount of information the non-verbal conveys; and methods and strategies to make use of this visual information to cue, scaffold, and support aural comprehension. In short, 'reading' and interpreting body language is part and parcel of being communicatively competent and video is a medium par excellence for building this visual competence. Paralinguistic subtleties can be frozen in time, studied, repeated, mimicked, and interpreted using videotape, videodisc, and/or digitized sequences stored on a computer.

Another form of visual competence is the ability to assess and categorize the visual elements of film, television, and video into categories or genres. This is a skill that media-saturated societies exercise as a matter of course as they encounter visual media. The skill of 'reading' visual information to augment comprehension of target language aural and textual material, moreover, can be trained to great advantage. With a minimum of awareness, we are capable of assessing and categorizing at a glance the type of video we are viewing: a dramatic reenactment, a talk show, reality TV, a documentary. Stepping back and becoming more aware of this automated reaction is a healthy exercise for all, particularly for language learners. The process and resulting awareness can assist and strengthen a learner's access and comprehension strategies. Learners can use this quick categorization skill to activate a useful schema that will assist them in comprehending the video. Learners can then exercise their existing knowledge in their quest to put together all incoming target language information and make sense of it in the immediate context. To some degree this means applying extant knowledge about and experiences with the medium. In another sense, thoroughly understanding target language messages implies a fairly good grasp of the social and cultural norms that apply to the ways the media presentation was produced, the way it is viewed within the target culture, and interpreted within that viewing culture. These socially agreed upon (often *de facto*) systems of representation (definitions, conventions, and associations) make up the interpretive frameworks for native speakers of the language and culture of presentation. They are integral to the complex of sociocultural, sociolinguistic realms in which the learner is expected to understand and operate.

Unpacking the means and methods of a video presentation is a healthy exercise, plain and simple. It enables us to be participants rather than passive recipients. For language learners it is activity that engages thinking about language and visual systems of communication as well as the subtleties and the power contained within them.

Pictures, Still and Moving

Visuals in the form of still pictures come in familiar forms and, for the most part, are readily accessible in our daily environment. Whether in their analog form – books, magazines, newspapers, flash cards – or in the digital form – pictures on the internet or stored on your computer – they share essential features. They

- represent
- illustrate
- evoke
- invite interpretation

They are, therefore, primary staples for language instruction, especially for beginners – linking new vocabulary with meaning while avoiding use of translation being standard practice. Used throughout language curricular levels, images are often used to anchor and generate communicative activity. In second language contexts where Sheltered* approaches are used to teach the target language through content, visual are a key tool in the Sheltered Language toolbox. In short, because the chief goal is to render concrete that which is otherwise abstract, visuals make good, solid sense in language education overall.

Video as Language Learning Material

The ancient cliché, "a picture is worth a thousand words," couldn't hit closer to home than for the video medium. For almost a century, the human mind has evolved the facility for processing not single pictures, but twenty-eight or thirty single pictures or frames *per second*. To place this in perspective, when 'moving pictures' were first experienced, the response was frequently an overwhelming fear—a reaction to the amount of visual information coming in and the frightening semblance of 'real life.' This lightening fast flow of single sequential images gets translated into meaningful representations of movement, action, and life. If one of those images in a thirtieth of a second is evocative of a thousand words (or in the language classroom arguably many more) then what does this exponentially augmented stream of visuals imply? And what of the corresponding aural component?

Some commonly highlighted features of video for language learning are:

- recorded video material provide controlled access to linguistic and paralinguistic detail and subtlety that otherwise can elude the language learner

- language is presented within the target culture

- language is visually contextualized

- language is communicatively contextualized (videos tell stories)

- video provides the opportunity to study representative slices of life in the target language and culture

- learners can exert control over rate and order of presentation

- learners can manipulate and reshape video to change meaning

- video offers clear enunciation (typically) of characters/speakers

- video dramatizes linkages between language and action

- video is intrinsically motivating

Beyond these commonly cited advantages for the medium, there is a world of possibilities for use of video sequences as a source and springboard for rich problem solving and analysis regarding presentation (craft), messages (content), and interpretation (the various readings they evoke).

Language Processing

As with the audio medium, video viewing was once considered a passive activity. It is now understood to be potentially quite active. Like reading and listening, much more is involved than the overly simplistic notion of a transmission of information. Active viewing implies that the mind is actively working on the symbol system in conjunction with many and diverse forms of prior and developing knowledge.

The video medium is comprised of simultaneous sight and sound. This translates into viewers engaging more than one perceptual modality at a time: seeing and listening. The medium brings together the visual and the aural into a unique text that, many have argued, increases comprehensibility due to the additional, complementary information the visual channel contributes to aural comprehension and vice versa. In this respect alone video is widely considered a medium well suited for language learning. Students have two parallel sets of information to use in decoding and comprehending what they view. Images on the screen provide powerful clues and cues to aural meaning. Beyond this defining characteristic, simultaneous sight and sound, there are additional attributes of the video medium that render it a powerful tool for learning language such as, genre schema, motivation, and general appeal.

The nature of this kind of language processing—that involved in viewing and comprehending video—can be seen as a powerful contribution to the second language acquisition process. Indeed, there is some evidence that regular viewing of target language television programming increases listening skills as well as overall proficiency in the new language (National Captioning Institute, 2000; Meskill, 1996). Anecdotally, in my own experience with ESL learners, many have reported that much of their learning of English came from watching television shows like *Sesame Street* and situation comedies at home on a regular basis (see Chapter 2). A Japanese friend swears she learned English from watching Sunday afternoon football games. Interestingly, after some twenty years in this country her English is still peppered with reportage style and imperative structures!

Video Literacy

Response to any medium is heavily mitigated by the extent of our prior experiences with it. In the case of video, the role the medium has come to play in the lives of all contemporary peoples is extensive. We can be sure that the majority of language students come to the learning process well versed in the medium and its conventions. They come literate and psychologically prepared to attend to and react to video using comprehension skills and strategies that they have developed over their lifetime. As a consequence of extensive prior experience, users are motivated by the medium as well as accustomed to decoding its messages for extended periods of time. In short, they come to the task of learning a new language *video literate*. These existing skills and strategies need not only be recognized and valued in the language classroom, but can also be capitalized on in instruction.

Video productions typically represent specific and familiar genres. As previously mentioned, learners are most likely familiar with these genres and their conventions. They are accomplished 'readers' of video narratives. Like stories in print, stories depicted in the video medium use specific conventions to represent characters, events, and feelings. In addition to the story itself, visual techniques work to focus and manipulate our attention and emotions as well. Language learners are versed in 'reading' these stories, if not also in recognizing the craft behind their production.

Genre conventions provide useful schemas that can serve viewers whose competency in understanding the aural code may be weak. Learning a new language, one can make use of prior knowledge of and experience with a genre to infer, predict, and make sense of what they are hearing in the target language. The situation comedy, for example, represents a "bare bones" genre: it is story in its most compact, decodable form. Situation comedy characters are not complicated. They are highly predictable. This contributes to the humor and charm of the genre. Moreover, the problems and the processes learners undergo to find their solutions are readily recognizable as they relate directly to everyday life. Their speech is clear, timed, and punctuated so that the joke, innuendo, or moral is easily accessed. For non-native speakers, such a stark, consistent schema serves to aid comprehensibility.

In short, the schema support inherent in conventional video genres is a great asset to the non-native speaker. Learners' familiarity with these standard forms and the direct relation between form and the content of characters and their activity can enhance this type of interaction with target language media. The following are just a few suggestions of how learners can be prompted to make use of their genre knowledge:

- Popular music videos are ballads of sorts; that is, they tell stories. In a very short time span (typically 2-3 minutes) a story or series of interlocking stories are told visually and aurally. As such they can be treated as literature to be analyzed, responded to, and subjected to various perspectives and interpretations.

- Television news programs, sometimes referred to as the 'masculine soap opera' (Fiske, 1987) is a richly compact genre. Many take controversial human interest stories to the extreme — dosing up reality with those elements of fiction that captivate us, at least long enough for us not to change the channel. Unpacking news presentations in terms of craft, agenda, message, and implications can involve language learners in high level communicative practice and exercise a range of very potent and useful language and thinking.

- Like television news shows, soap operas and reality TV are also jam-packed with intrigue, lust, obsession, and grief. The melodramatic quality of the genre, however, renders soaps even more comprehensible than the news. Body language and affect give clear indications of intention. Viewing a short segment with no sound and inferring from the visual what is being said is a powerful learning activity. Learners can benefit a great deal from using soaps to 'read' the body language of the target culture while being swept up in raw issues characteristic of these shows.

The video medium is as pervasive as it is in our daily lives for a simple reason: we enjoy it. It is the primary medium we turn to for entertainment, information, and recreation. Its appeal lies in visually sophisticated materials, the intriguing techniques used to present them, the content that gets treated, and the relative ease with which we access and process what we view.

Given learners' extensive experience watching and successfully reading the text of video, we can assume that they are, after years of viewing, confident with the medium. This confidence can be bolstered for and through target language instruction. If learners are confident about watching video in the target language, then they will watch. They can be empowered through the sense of confidence derived from not only comprehending but also enjoying programming in the target language. Empowerment and confidence spells increased motivation to learn.

Some useful criteria for assessing the motivational value of a video can be borrowed from the realm of reading. Anderson, Shirley, Wilson and Fielding (1986) outline the following as criteria for readers to be involved in what they read:

- identification with characters: if readers identify with characters, they will consequently become interested in their thoughts and actions

- novelty: novel content promotes interest and involvement

- life-themes: interest is generated through themes that are relevant to readers' own lives

- level of activity: the intensity of actions and emotions is in direct proportion to levels of involvement

- background knowledge: sufficient background knowledge is required for involvement

Video that motivates and engages viewers shares these same features.

Story

Underlying blockbuster films and *Sesame Street* are the ties that bind: story – its basic anatomy, character types and roles, the unfolding of events, the mirror and manipulation of being human. It's unfortunate that where film and television are excellent story-telling vehicles, initial attempts at utilizing story in instructional videos were stilted and oftentimes silly. Their production budgets, which translate into caliber of talent, writing, and production quality, were 'educational,' not Hollywood blockbuster. A breakthrough occurred in conceiving the technology as offering possibilities beyond perpetuating the sage-on-the-stage tradition. It was only a matter of time, and a great deal of money, that instruction through the video medium would rise to new artistic heights, would, like the entertainment industry, push the technology envelope to make stories ever more engaging.

In the nineteen sixties, the Public Broadcasting Service (PBS), through the Children's Television Workshop, made a huge conceptual breakthrough regarding video/TV and learning. Workshop developers recognized and acted on the fact that people respond much more to fully developed characters and stories than to the straight exposition that had traditionally been the format and flavor of instructional materials. Where talking heads with a few scholarly props in the background had been the standard for educational video, with *Sesame Street* and the *Electric Company* came lively, charming characters with full lives and intrigue, whose interaction in engaging plots involves viewers still in learning letters, numbers, and life lessons. In short, PBS began viewing the medium as a vehicle for telling stories and it is arguably through stories that we learn best.

The downside of the use of story is the manufacturing of public attitude, opinion, and attempted maintenance of mass mores, which has, according to many media and social critics, reached new heights. Manipulation of the public through crafted media messages is pervasive and very effective. The evening news keeps us anxious, and anxiety is good for the economy. Primetime situation comedies provide a warm and fuzzy sense of belonging to fictitious microworlds manufactured for that very purpose. We watch them (and their commercial breaks) with rapt attention (Rushkoff, 1996).

Take, for example, the following laundry list of Tad Friend's tried and true rules for the construction of the situation comedy. If you've ever watched a situation comedy, you will quickly recognize these elements.

> The rules run more or less as follows: shows have an A story and a subsidiary, or B, story (and sometimes a C story as well), which are "broken" across a "teaser" and two acts; scenes should have three laughs to a page; no character can leave a room without saying something funny; and a scene should end with a zinger that sends everyone into the commercial laughing. (For example, two characters ask the boss for a raise, the boss yells and storms out, and one character says brightly, "Well that went well.") This is the "button," or "blow," to the scene. Sitcom characters also behave in predictably eccentric ways: they sit around three sides of a dinner table (leaving one side for the camera); are always best friends with people across the hall; spend every night having strangely audible conversations with their friends in strangely uncrowded bars; refer to sex with bizarre euphemisms ("She really rotated my tires!"); speak expositorily on the phone ("I know you're my mother, and you just want to remind me that my brother Jonathan is allergic to cats"); run amok with new responsibilities until they're "drunk with power"; get embroiled in weird misunderstandings and, instead of just explaining the confusion, break into someone's apartment to replace the message they'd left on the answering machines; never do any actual work; often learn lessons that require a group hug; and never watch TV themselves. (Friend, 1998, p.79)

Where tried and true formulae are the stuff of crafting commercial media, they are also the stuff that make a good story in general. Video is representational; what you see and hear is the tale. Unlike great literature, commercial media is crafted for the masses and as such stays away from counting on viewers to imagine and infer very much. Sitting down to be entertained, even informed, excludes the desire to do work, to think, to exert effort beyond clicking the remote or fisting up some popcorn.

TV news has come to follow the 'no effort' maxim in their packaging and delivery as well. Mainstream news is now reduced to the simplest units; the sound bite, pictures and slogans tell whole, complex stories, thus relieving the burden of thought from the consumer. In the film, *Wag the Dog*, for example, a feigned U.S. attack on Albania was crafted into four static images and a slogan: a white cat, a photograph of a POW with Morse code snagged on the front of his sweater, old shoes strung on trees and lampposts, a flag-draped coffin, and the slogan *Come Home, Old Shoe*. These simple codes—all artifices of visual and aural craft manufactured for minds desiring only the least common denominator against which to pit their emotions of loyalty and narcissism—got quickly appropriated by the public. The film did a brilliant job in pointing out how for each war – arguably the most devastatingly complex of human activity – there is a representation or image in our minds that says it all. Arlington National Cemetery, the statue of Iwo Jima, Rosie the Riveter, a Vietnamese civilian engulfed in flames, the evil Saddam, the villain bin Laden. These serve to render what is painfully complex and unconscionable into sterile, quickly digestible morsels.

Understanding the Craft

The stories told through film and video are representationally distinct from those told through other means. Where you may think such visual systems are seemingly unlimited, they are in fact closed systems as far as the stories they can tell and the syntax and semantics used in the telling goes. Just as story has a limited number of basic structures, the camera has a limited number of angles. The video 'author' uses a limited number of options in combination to make the story come to life.

Just as craft is what makes a good story, craft is what makes a good video. However, without a good story, even the hottest video special effects and fancy camera work can flop. Take as examples these two stories:

> Story 1
> *For a number of centuries, study of Latin texts was restricted to the elite. Translation tasks were assigned to young male charges by their strict tutors.*
>
> - passive voice
> - abstract references
> - absent/distant characters

A literal visual rendering of the story as told here would consist of a talking head and perhaps an omniscient shot of a tutor and tutees studying their Latin texts.

> Story 2
> *Randal Tomey finished off his porridge, grabbed up his slate and quill and hurried off to the monastery. Brother Kinney stood at the entrance of the cell and demanded: "Let me see your Latin translations..."*
>
> - real people
> - active voice

- eating creates intimacy/identification with character
- motives present
- conflict (time, agenda)
- resolution (arrival)
- suspense

Even without a video rendering, Story 2 is more memorable, engaging, evocative, visual, and, consequently, more educative. You have most likely made your own video of the story in your head.

Story as a Second Language

The story and craft of the video medium are important fundamental concepts for language learners in two regards.

1) Understanding the medium, its craft, and how its messages get constructed is, in fact, learning another language. As such, understanding video provides an additional system of understanding as an aid to making sense of the target language and culture. In addition, understanding video helps us better understand ourselves and our society as media consumers.

2) Coming to understand the workings of the medium and exercising what one already knows about the medium (see Chapter 2) lay the groundwork for taking charge of it.

In terms of video in language education, the traditional mantra (viz., recorded audio and video provide controlled access to linguistic and paralinguistic detail—access to the subtleties of language and culture that can elude learners in live contexts) has solid pedagogical rationale. Controlling how one samples and studies a target language by using recordings of it makes sense for learning and teaching.

DITIGAL STORYTELLING AND IDENTITY TEXTS

Stories are not limited to commercial production. Before television, prior to motion pictures, and even before written language, came oral stories. It is an age-old human tradition, and each student has her own, unique stories to tell. The story formulae used in commercial production can be easily applied to stories your students create. Digital stories are created with computer software or Internet sites using images, spoken dialogue, audio, and even text, arranged in a specific order and saved as a video file.

The result can be a spectacular display of language production that is personally motivating to learners. More importantly, digital stories contain all of the elements of Communication, Form, and Affect discussed in the previous chapters; that is, the activities are focused, personal opportunities for the students to learn and exercise their new L2 voices. Because they are task specific, they provide students with attainable goals in their language learning. Digital Storytelling activities can be completed by one student or small groups.

Taking the notion one step further, digital stories are a form of *identity text* (Cummins, 2007) whereby students invest their *identities* in their products. A central argument in the use of identity texts is that instruction of all forms, including language instruction, is effective inasmuch as it "affirms [learner] identities and enables them to invest their identities in learning" (Cummins et. al., 2005, p. 40). Some of the features of identity texts are:

- they build on students cultural and linguistic capital
- they explicitly assist in developing content knowledge (in this case, target language)
- they enable learners to construct knowledge

Identity texts tie nicely into Cummins's discussions of oral histories, where students connect their personal lives to their learning through collecting information about their past.

Linking these two ideas back to digital storytelling, digital stories can be used in the production of autobiographies, presentations, narratives, and other stories to share with peers. One potential for digital storytelling is having students create stories which provide information on their culture. This is a highly enticing concept as they are personal to students and thereby provide an opportunity for them to meaningfully utilize the target language in a goal-focused context, and provide students opportunities to teach each other. Students can decide on what they would like to teach, select images that will appropriately represent their 'lesson', write a script, assemble the 'story', record the themselves describing the cultural notable and compile the story to share with others. Practical use of the language with the teacher present to provide form-focused feedback can foster student acquisition of language.

See the Appendix for a list of digital storytelling resources.

USING VIDEO IN THE CLASSROOM

The first rule of thumb when conceptualizing the use of video in the classroom is:

the shorter the better

Attention spans aren't what they used to be. The trend in The Media, and what we have become accustomed to, is short, quick packages of visual and auditory information. The best method for selecting off-air recorded segments to use with your class is to locate professional or amateur videos on the internet. If you can't find what you'd like, you can record from your television. Look for *short*, usable segments. Remember, if you want students to simply watch, they can do this on their own time as an assignment. Valuable class time should be spent in *active* comprehension and production that involves interaction and instruction, not in passive viewing.

The second rule is: the video segment that you choose as material needs to be *self-contained*. There is nothing more frustrating to seasoned video viewers (your students) than having a story line cut off (the pause button hit) midstream during what was designed to be viewed as a whole. While there may at some point be a solid pedagogical reason to do this (e.g., having learners predict what will happen next), it is, for the most part, irritating. Starting and stopping runs counter to our habits of involvement with the story being presented. Don't despair, though; *self-contained* can be very broadly defined. It can mean a still frame from a recorded video off of which learners can discover new vocabulary, create dialog, story, backgrounds and agendas of characters. *Self-contained* can mean a 15-second commercial that learners can unpack, deconstruct, analyze, discover agendas for, and discuss in its sociopolitical/cultural context. *Self-contained* can mean a segment from a situation comedy or soap opera that has sufficient information provided before viewing or while viewing for learners to be satisfied.

Co-viewing, Co-constructing Meaning

The term *co-viewing* (viewing with other students and teacher) as used here contrasts radically with the video-device-wheeled-into-the-room-and-lights-off scenario common of video use in the classroom. Co-viewing is purposeful viewing in consort with others with whom analysis, meaning, and interpretation is undertaken. The richness and success of these collaborative processes are highly dependent on the quality of the tasks assigned and implemented.

Pre-viewing

Pre-viewing tasks and activities can be just as lively, interactive, and supportive of language practice as the viewing process itself, if not more. Pre-viewing tasks also serve to render the viewing experience a more active and accessible one.

Summary Preview
Perhaps the most facilitative pre-viewing task is to have students read and/or listen to a summary of the video's content in advance of viewing. The summary can contain a complete skeletal picture of what will be viewed if the material is particularly challenging. Omitting key information from the summary, though, can add an element of surprise and delight at discovery. Learners can thereby discover new information for which they have been primed in the summary.

Vocabulary Preview
The pre-teaching of vocabulary words that will occur in the video segment can certainly activate learner awareness of new words as they are used in highly contextualized situations. Attention drawn to specific new vocabulary items can support comprehension and recycled *use* of those items in later activities.

Viewing Questions
Compile a list of questions for learners to review and discuss prior to viewing. These can be straightforward and informational or you may chose to use chunquing to fashion focus on particular language/culture elements. If, for example, the segment contains repeated use of a particular syntactic form, idiomatic expression, or language function, attention to these may be drawn through questions have learners review and prepare to answer prior to viewing.

Directed Viewing
Give learners a brief list of key points to which you'd like them to pay special attention. They can be discussed and clarified in detail prior to viewing.

Flow Charts
To assist learners in making sense of their viewing experience, provide a set of sketches or a flow chart representing the content and action in the segment they will view. Again, you can leave some of the blocks in these

sketch series or flow charts blank and have learners complete them based on the video.

Pre-view follow-ups
As part of pre-viewing activity, describe for your students the kinds of activities they will engage in once they have viewed the segment.

While-viewing

In addition to paying special attention to features introduced during pre-viewing activities, learners can be asked to undertake while-viewing activities. Doing something while viewing naturally adds to the active nature of their viewing and, in many cases, the amount of investment learners will make in the experience.

Predictions
As mentioned earlier, segments selected should be in some way self-contained with pausing avoided if the flow of action risks being interrupted. If learners are alerted to the rationale behind pauses in advance, however, the method of 'pause for prediction' can be very engaging. As an alternative to the teacher making decisions as to when to pause the video and ask what will happen next, a student can be assigned the remote control and take charge of the activity.

Paper Work
Although it is cumbersome to ask students to write and watch a video at the same time, there may be instances where giving them a chart to complete, a map to follow, a diagram to alter, or characters to identify on paper makes sense. Be sure they have a chance to look at both the video and the paper thoroughly before asking them to complete the written work while viewing.

Interactive Viewing
Starting and stopping a videotape can also be an effective technique when implementing an interactive viewing task. Here a segment is played of someone speaking, the video is paused, and students are asked to speak out loud a line of dialog that would make sense as a reply to the character in the video segment. If more than one viable suggestion is offered, each can be recorded (written down or audiotaped), the video's response played in turn, and a comparison made of students' versus the videotape's utterance.

Role Play
You can take interactive viewing one step further and have individual learners take on the roles of characters in the segment. Not only does a learner provide his or her character's line when the tape is paused, but delivers the line dramatically, in keeping with the character in the video.

Post-viewing

All of the above potentially provide focus and material for post-viewing activities. Indeed, debriefing on the tasks learners undertake before and during viewing is a must. Beyond reviewing, compiling, comparing, and discussing, any number of expansion or springboard activities can be undertaken that provide additional practice with the language and concepts worked on through the video segment.

VIDEO IN CLASS AND OUT

Chapter 2 discusses correspondences between in-class and out-of-class viewing as well as the importance of building on learners' shared knowledges, experiences, and interests. It seems everyone watches TV or films at some point during their daily or weekly routine. For language learners, this can represent contact with the target language and culture. As was pointed out earlier, this contact carries many implications regarding acquisition of the language and developing an understanding of the target culture.

In considering classroom use of off-air television recordings, out-of-class contact with the medium is important to keep in mind. Also important are the television literacy skills that language learners develop having watched television for a good part of their lives in their native language. These literacy skills (e.g., understanding television broadcast genres, camera angle and movement conventions, plot, action, and character development) can be highlighted as useful strategies students can use to help them understand the aural portion of the video medium.

The following are additional suggestions for training learners to make productive use of their in and/or out of class viewing time.

- During/directly after a one-half hour show, jot down 3 versions of its plot (class assignment for which students' work can be compared, contrasted, and discussed).

- Watch with the sound off and write a description of what you believe is happening. Then watch with the sound on, write a description, and compare your interpretations.

- Write down, or draw, five gestures you notice during the course of a half-hour show. State what they mean.

- On a horizontal time line, plot out the events of a show as you watch. Draw, or jot down, events along the line as they happen. When events are not chronological, accommodate this in your picture.

- Stop a previously unseen but recorded show periodically and write down predictions as to what will happen next. Compare the prediction with what really happens in the show. Be prepared to state how you knew this.

- Before viewing, talk with others or read a description to give you an idea about the show's genre. Think about other shows you have seen, plays you have attended, or books you have read that have similar plots and themes. In other words, come to viewing with a well defined set of expectations regarding what you will watch, and how it will be constructed.

- Record a half-hour show. Using the fast forward button, scan it without sound. Write down your predictions of plot and action based on the scan. Watch the show in normal play mode and compare your predictions to the actual content. What percentage was comprehensible from the visual only? What kinds of detail/information did the aural fill in for you?

- Listen to a show without looking at the screen. Watch again while looking at the screen. Compare the internal visual images you generated to what you see when you view the show.

- Practice new listening and repeating strategies. Based on the visual portion of a recorded video segment, decide before replaying what aural component to listen for. This could be a word, a phrase, the gist, the intonation, or another feature.

- Embellish what you have viewed by rewriting the plot. Compare your new version with those of your classmates.

CLOSED CAPTIONING

Closed captioning is widely available for television. In the U.S., for example, all televisions manufactured after 1993 were required by law to have closed captioning capability. In 2006, the Federal Communications Commission mandated that all new English language programs, with limited exceptions, be close captioned (Federal Communications Commission, 2009). Many cable companies offer closed captioning boxes that provide captioning in several languages. This means that you could watch the movie *Titanic* or *The Price is Right* with, for example, Japanese or Arabic captions. If your students have this capability, encourage them to make use of captioning while viewing at home or in a school laboratory.

Recorded shows that have captions in the target language can work well in the classroom as well. Be aware that you must both record and playback a captioned segment on units that have captioning. If you record from a unit that has captioning, this does not automatically mean it will play back with captions if the playback setup does not have caption decoding capability. In the classroom, captioned segments can be freeze-framed for close study of the written version of the aural text, blocked out on first viewing and revealed during the second, used as a cloze test check, or read aloud by students with the video's sound off.

COMPREHENSIBILITY VS. AUTHENTICITY

Like audio clips, the trend in language video design was originally to simplify and sanitize the target language, the rationale being that one hundred percent comprehensibility was tantamount in learning language. Thus, there are a number of commercial videos that depict speakers speaking scripts s-l-o-w-l-y and unnaturally. Likewise, there are exaggerated pauses between speaker lines, something that is again quite alien to native speaker interaction. (Pauses carry quite a bit a meaning, and when placed for no meaning related to the conversation, are odd, especially in U.S. culture where silences in conversations are awkward and uncomfortable.) Of course, there are arguments for and against simplifying the language of video. When the aural text is challenging to the point that students become overwhelmed and lose confidence and motivation, and the assigned task cannot be modified to allow them some form of success, there is a problem. As with audio clips, the trend to pare back on language complexity seems to be subsiding and materials developers are now considering scripting and casting their video scenes so that authenticity is not sacrificed. On the computer, the speed at which digital audio and video is played can be controlled (i.e., slowed down or sped up) thereby increasing both comprehensibility while maintaining authenticity.

SUMMARY

Where the often manipulative agenda of the video-viewing experience is potentially dangerous, it is nonetheless a feature that can act positively on the learning process. It motivates sustained attending, it touches us deeply, and it provokes connections in our minds between content (characters, events, locales) and our own real life experiences. Video content is, moreover, explicitly geared towards this evocation and relevance for viewers. In other words, we can suspend disbelief and become thoroughly engaged and even engrossed. At the same time, as critical consumers, we can step back and reflect on the responses we have.

Video opens up numerous possibilities for the teaching of critical viewing skills while focusing at the same time on structures, functions, vocabulary, non-verbal communication, culture, and the like. Mining the richness of the medium for these multiple dimensions of the language curricula is an adventure you'll enjoy undertaking.

END OF CHAPTER NOTE: EXPLOITING THE MEDIUM

One time when I was visiting an EFL classroom in Egypt, students were given the opportunity to express their views regarding their EFL course materials. Many sang the praises of the audio cassette player their instructor had recently been using in class. They had been listening to the tapes that accompanied their text and workbooks, both of which focused on grammar- and function- based dialogues. These tapes brought new native speaker voices into the classroom. They were praised by the students, who lamented their lack of contact with native speakers, something they felt strongly would greatly benefit their English. In the context of expressing great pleasure at being able to listen to 'authentic' language (these were highly scripted, commercially produced language learning tapes), one student began to complain about their school not having a language laboratory. "We could benefit so much from listening to more native English!" he cried.

I thought for a moment about these students, who they were, what their lives were like. The director of the school had told me that these adult students made tremendous sacrifices, traveled long distances, and had to wedge English study time into demanding family and professional schedules. Where could they fit in this native speaker contact they so desired? I also recalled that the entire country came to a screeching halt in the evenings as Egyptians from every walk of life, every corner of the country, hovered around their television sets. The U.S. serial drama, *The Bold and the Beautiful*, had taken the country by storm. Broadcast daily during primetime, the series had captivated family evening hours and much casual conversation before, during, and after the show aired. Men and women throughout the nation were watching and listening (programs were subtitled in Arabic) to native speakers of English—albeit melodramatic ones—every weekday night right in their own homes!

In response to the students' complaints about no language lab, I brought up the *Bold and the Beautiful* phenomenon with the class. "Aren't there native speakers in your living room every evening?" I challenged. After some thought and conferencing, there was a nodding of heads. We went on to talk about ways they could take advantage of that 'language laboratory' in their living rooms. They could tape episodes if they or a neighbor had a VCR for stopping, starting, repeating. They could Scotch-tape paper over the subtitles to practice their comprehension. And, rather than talking about the latest turns of event in Arabic, they could use some of the English vocabulary, phrases, and expressions they had heard when conversing with their colleagues about the show. They seemed satisfied with this method of native speaker contact. I have since heard reports that EFL teachers are encouraging these practices with their students and making use of this out-of-class 'contact' with native speakers for teaching the language.

Activities

Discussion

On the business side of video, TV, and film production there are, of course, a range of strata. What we experience most often in our daily lives—and what we export as depictions of ourselves to other nations—is on the highest investment end, which translates into the highest production quality. The television, film, and video rental industries are huge money makers. At the heart of profit is the art and artifice of telling a good story. As much as special effects—'eye candy' in the industry—can get our blood thumping, it is *story* that ultimately makes or breaks the viewing experience.

Discuss a film or television production you've seen recently in term of this two-tiered notion of quality:

1) the production (glitz) value, and
2) the story

Contrast two or three and see how they 'weigh in' as popular media.

Visually Reading the Meaning

Spend ten minutes watching a random television program with the sound off. Spend another ten minutes observing people interact with one another in a public place where you can see, but not hear, the interlocutors. Which 10 minutes supplied the most information? Why do you think?

Fortune Lines

Have students visually plot the story in a video of their choice (off-air programming or other). Review how to stop, start, rewind, and scan the video medium being used. Select a concept that may be prominent or buried in the given story: anger, job, worry, obsession, lightheartedness, and the like. Plot out the evolution of the story one concept at a time. The story of Little Red Riding Hood, for example, when plotted out for **fear** would look something like this:

leaves home	enters forest	meets stranger (wolf)	arrives at grand-mother's	talks to grandmother
___	___	___	___	___

The thinking and discussion that goes on in the process of doing these kinds of fortune lines is quite rich. So too is the language used in generating the explication for lines going up and down within a story. Attention is drawn to the forms stories take and the language of stories is practiced in an engaging way.

Regarding Network Websites

Network websites offer a wealth of teaching ideas and supplementary materials across a range of subjects:

ABC: http://www.abc.com
NBC: http://www.nbc.com
CBS: http://www.cbs.com
FOX: http://www.fox.com
Public Broadcasting Station: http://www.pbs.org

Regarding Cable in the Classroom

http://www.ciconline.com

Regarding Online Video Sites

YouTube: http://www.youtube.com/
Online Video Guide: http://www.ovguide.com/

Regarding Making and Storing Your Own Videos

http://clear.msu.edu/clear/

Digital Storytelling
Center for Digital Storytelling
http://www.storycenter.org/

Digital Storytelling @ LaGuardia
http://www.lagcc.cuny.edu/ctl/dstory/default.htm

Voice Thread
http://voicethread.com/#home
This online site allows students to create and share their digital stories.

Additional Reading on Digital Storytelling

Bull, G., & Kajder, S. (2004). Digital storytelling in the language arts classroom. *Learning and Leading with Technology*, 32(4), 46-49. Available online at http://cs2.cust.educ.ubc.ca/csed/400/csed_readings/display%2024.pdf

6. Computers in Language Learning: From Constructed to Constructing

> *A TV screen or computer monitor cannot be thought of simply as an object to be looked at, with all the old forms of psychic projection and investment; instead, the screen intersects responsively with our desires and representations, and becomes the embodied form of our psychic worlds. What happens "on" the screen is neither on the screen nor in us, but in some complex, always virtual space between the two.*
>
> (Connor, 1989)

It's a chilly Tuesday morning in mid-February. Mrs. Watts' third-grade class is just settling down for their daily language arts lesson. The children's chatter fades as they go to their desks and take out books and pencils.

A dark-haired child with skin the color of maple has been seated at her desk since entering the classroom. She is watching the others as they move around the room and socialize. Her wide eyes study her classmates. Mrs. Watts stands at the blackboard, chalk in hand. "Page 47, please." she says as she begins to write a sample sentence on the board. The children flip through their books to find the correct page. María continues to watch. Mrs. Watts turns from the board to check that all are on the right page. She notices María sitting mute, attentive, with no book in front of her.

She has no book, Mrs. Watts remembers. María had just come to this class the week before and, because no one was quite sure what to do with her, had been assigned a classroom and a seat, but no materials. A district specialist had tested María. She apparently spoke no English. No one seemed to know quite what to do with her.

Mrs. Watts remembered a suggestion made by the school librarian in the lunchroom when they had been discussing María. The librarian had suggested putting María on the classroom's computer. The school had purchased a software package designed for ESL learners. Mrs. Watts was welcome to borrow this for María to use until she learned enough English to participate in regular class activities.

Mrs. Watts places her chalk on the rim of the board and approaches María's desk. The child's eyes grow wider; she lowers them as the teacher comes near. Mrs. Watts motions to María. María obeys and follows the teacher to the back of the room where the classroom computer is set up. Mrs. Watts starts up the ESL software, shows María how to click on the first lesson, and returns to her place in front of the class. María, intent on pleasing the teacher, clicks as she has been shown. Pictures of animals appear on the screen. One by one she clicks on the names she guesses go with each image. A little chime sounds after each correct selection. A buzz indicates she should try again. After successfully choosing the word for three animals, she stealthily glances back at the rest of the class. They are engaged in lively talk with the teacher and each other while they work through the exercises on the board and in their books. María turns back to her animals, clicks on a few more words, then sneaks another longing look at her peers.

On another side of town...
That same morning, a combined second and third-grade classroom, in a district adjoining that of María's school, is also buzzing with activity. María's cousin, Lilia, is seated with a group comprised of both native speakers and non-native speakers of English. Along with María, Lilia has just arrived in the U.S. and speaks no English. Yet, she smiles and laughs as she looks intently at the others who are gesturing and repeating to her and to each other. This group is working around a computer screen where they see a half dozen pictures. Their job is to decide what order to put the pictures in, then compose a story about them. The children, including the non-native speakers, are excited and animated. They gesture at the screen and at each other. Lilia points to a picture and holds up one finger—"First! Yeah, that's first." cries one child. Lilia smiles and repeats "first." "Yes!" replies another child. "Yes!" Lilia joyfully repeats. Once the group has reached a consensus on a good order for the pictures, they assign one of the ESL learners to take dictation on the keyboard. Lilia has been put in charge of pointing out the pictures as they are discussed. A native speaker is to watch for spelling. Another acts as council and makes sure the group stays on task.

Your reaction...
Both María's and Lilia's classrooms will be discussed throughout this chapter. Before continuing, please jot down 1-3 words that describe your reaction to each of these scenarios:

María's classroom	Lilia's classroom

In trying to make sense of the forces that shape both the software (the same software package is used in both classrooms) and how that software gets used for language learning, let's first look at a bit of history.

COMPUTERS AND LEARNING: A BRIEF HISTORY

In the early 1970's the practicality of computers for instruction was rapidly becoming a reality. Consequently a great deal of software development took place. Initial design for Computer Assisted Instruction (CAI) was based on what computers do best: provide users with responses to their input. This stimulus-response role of the computer in instruction prevailed and continues to play a determining role in both how software is designed and used for learning.

In the early days, a user's input was limited to a keystroke or series of keystrokes; corresponding output from the computer was generated from simple algorithms that determined an appropriate response based on a user's input. This is essentially what computers are good at.

Computers were, and basically still are, simple machines. They can easily be programmed to display words or pictures on the screen in response to a user's action at the keyboard. The human-computer dialogues designed to occur in instructional software have essentially evolved according to this basic computing feature. The most common manifestation was and still is a format for machine-user conversation that looks like this:

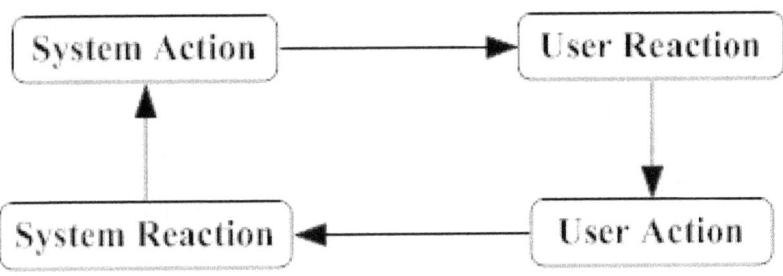

System Action
The computer displays a question or other form of decision on the screen with options for the user to respond. This can be in the form of a question, icon, or instructions of some kind.

Example: System acts—"What is the capital of the People's Republic of China?"
        "A. Baghdad
        B. Beijing
        C. Grenoble"

User Reaction
The user reacts to system action by making a decision.
   Example: User processes

User Action
The user makes a selection from options provided on the screen based on that decision.
   Example: User acts — "B"

System Reaction
The computer attempts to match the user's selection with a preprogrammed one.
   Example: System processes

System Action
The system then provides an action in keeping with its reaction to the user's action.
   Example: System acts — "Good" — and displays new question.

This framework for "dialogue" between machine and learner has formed the basis of most machine-user software design in general, and software design for instruction in particular. Instances where this dialogue format continues to be quite prevalent are found in the military and business sectors. Both have a distinct need for, and have in turn capitalized on, this form of dialogue in the training of knowledge sets and procedures. Individual trainees can drill and test themselves on facts and procedures pertinent to their professional work. When this learning is done via computer, training becomes more cost effective than gathering groups of learners in one place and hiring a trainer. There is also some evidence that training takes less time overall when the pace and sequence of instruction is determined by the individual trainee working on a computer.

This basic human-machine conversation has served as the basis not only for instructional software design in general but was also particularly appealing for foreign language study. There seemed to be an intuitive match between what is commonly perceived as the power of computing (this "conversation") and a language learner's need for practice with the target language. The earliest days of Computer Assisted Instruction consequently saw a flurry of excitement and initiatives around making the most of this match. Learners of another language, it was argued, need self-paced, tailored practice with the language they are learning. They need individualized practice beyond the classroom where, in large classes, they have limited opportunity to practice and self-test new vocabulary and grammar. The computer was and still is seen as a logical means of providing much needed practice beyond what happens in the language classroom. This form of practice, moreover, seemed to be able to suit individual learning needs and styles, something otherwise unlikely in mixed styles and abilities classrooms. In short, dialoguing with the machine by selecting responses to questions and receiving feedback was seen as a very attractive form of language practice.

COMPUTER ASSISTED LANGUAGE LEARNING (CALL) SOFTWARE

Early development of language learning software was largely based on the simple input-output model of instruction. They simply did what computers did best. Computers, being binary machines, were programmed to cue human input and to respond given a limited set of rules or criteria. For example, a learner is asked to fill in blanks or choose multiple choice answers to prompts or questions. Attached to these anticipated forms of learner input are output, or what has been popularly termed "feedback" messages of the *Very good* (María's chimes)/ *No, that's not it* (María's buzz) genre. Using this type of software, individual learners made their way through pages of workbook-like drills, achieved "mastery" at a given level, and moved on along a preprogrammed route. Tests and exercises tended to focus on the form of the target language—the mastery of grammatical structures from simple to more complex—and vocabulary—recognition, definition, and spelling.

Support for this genre of CALL was, and still is, that learners can "work at their own pace" and receive "immediate feedback" on their performance. Because mastery can be tracked by the computer as learners move from one level of difficulty to another, individuals can gain a sense of their progress and achievement based on their responses to on-line exercises and tests (María could learn how many animal names she correctly selected). Later versions of this type of software even have teacher management tools so the progress of individual students can be formally monitored and incorporated into learners' off-line progress reports.

Over the past three decades the range of instructional approaches to CALL software development has certainly expanded. However, the underlying structure of the system-user dialogue continues to be the basic building block. Instructional design approaches have expanded in response to the increased processing capabilities of personal computers and to pedagogical advances and innovation. Along with the fairly drastic changes in thinking about the nature of teaching and learning have come software products that attempt to reflect these: e.g., discovery learning, whole language, portfolio assessments, and the like. In second language instruction, many commercial products reflect attempts to reconcile the goals and procedures involved in Communicative Language Teaching and the limitations of current technologies—what computers can and can't do. Both of these issues—CLT and the strengths and limitations of current computer processing capabilities—are discussed in later sections.

The figure below represents a typology of tasks typical to CALL software design. Tasks appear aligned to the two continua: plus or minus content (vertical), and transmitted versus mediated learning (horizontal). Placement of each software type represents its proximity to being rich or poor in content:

- representations of real, motivated uses of the target language versus discrete, decontextualized units and how the task aligns with a transmitted versus mediated approach to learning;

- transmission of information through the basic system-user dialogue, versus open-ended environments that entail more thinking and involvement on the part of the learner.

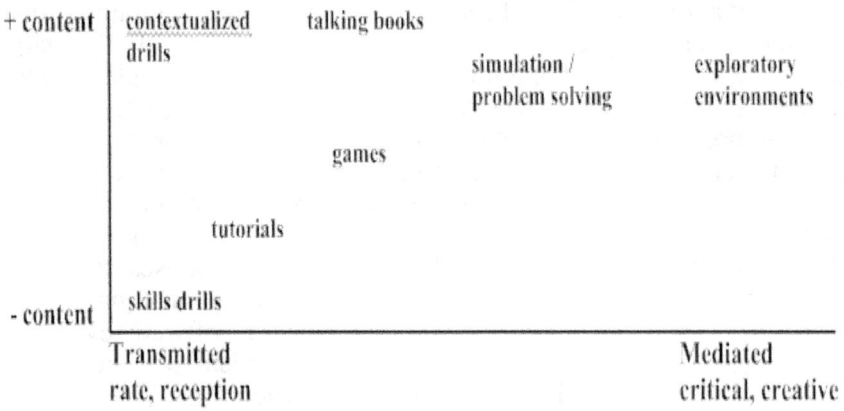

Figure 6.1. Types of CALL Learning Tasks

A common definition of the term **drills** involves exercises that support the memorization of discrete facts. In the case of language learning, this would mean memorization of vocabulary items, specific rules and structures, and the like. As indicated in Figure 6.1, drills can be devoid of content (lower left corner). Typically these are "skills drills": multiple choice and fill in the blank for sentences unrelated by meaning to one another. In other words, language appears in a format that emphasizes Form over meaning. Drills can also be contextualized (upper left corner above) as when multiple choice and fill in the blanks for sentences are related by meaning. In this case, sentences tell a cohesive story, or provide a coherent description.

Much like textbooks, **tutorials** are screens in a software package that explain or teach by providing information and examples. They are relatively rich in content of a sort, mostly explications and examples. But as far as representing the ways in which language is truly used as Communication, tutorials can, but don't necessarily, include this dimension. They might, for example, display grammar rules accompanied by examples using artificial sentences or dialogues. This software type therefore appears mid-point on the four axes. Tutorials are potentially rich in content (though very often are not) and are by nature transmission-oriented.

Games can be just as transmission-oriented and content poor as some skills drills. The learner may simply be responding to multiple choice and fill in exercises that have some gaming element built in: for example, a rabbit moving closer to a carrot for each correct answer, or scoring with bells or beeps. This genre of gaming task is not only potentially content poor, but also reflects more of a transmitted than a mediated approach to learning. There are games, however, that are both content rich and that use a mediated approach. These are more often designed for native speakers, something that will be discussed in a later section. For the most part language-specific software games heavily emphasize Form. Target language structures are represented in contrived and sanitized contexts and therefore tend toward content-poor, transmission orientations.

Very rich in content are **Talking Books**. Though the majority of talking books are produced for native speakers, this genre of software has been long touted and used as a genre of software well suited for language learners (e.g., Meskill & Swan, 1997). Talking Books are series of computer screens that resemble pages of illustrated books. As the learner looks at these illustrations, she can also read and hear the text of the story, click on unfamiliar words for definitions and, in some cases, get translations of words into other languages. Some Talking Books also offer "special clickables"—portions of the illustration that when clicked respond with special sounds and animations. 'Reading' Talking Books can be viewed as a content-rich task; there is, after all, a story and illustrations that publishers have deemed sufficiently motivating to make commercially available in this format. As far as the pedagogical boundaries of transmitted versus mediated are concerned, there are two ways to view the role of Talking Books. One is that the language and information of the text is in effect "transmitted" to the student by virtue of its popping out of the screen. In other words, the format renders the reading experience a place for a single, uncritical, unnegotiated experience of the story. On the other hand, with proper orchestration of this contact with Talking Books (see *Crafting Contexts for Use* later in this chapter), activity with this form of material can be rendered a mediated experience. The placement of Talking Books midway between the two approaches reflects this.

Simulations are computer-represented environments within which the learner is required to make decisions. In most cases, this decision-making involves problem solving through consideration of a variety of variables and a range of context-dependent information. Take for example a text adventure where the user must navigate a simulated world, collect objects, and pursue leads in order to complete a quest. In order to be successful, the learner must carefully consider a number of factors prior to every move. Since the environment is in the target language, the processing of this environmental information, thinking through, and responding to this information, involves active use of the target language. Engaging in simulations is, therefore, a mediated language task, one that requires critical and creative thinking using the target language.

Since first coined by John Higgins, **exploratory CALL** has been widely promoted for its apparent match with the philosophy, goals, and processes involved in Communicative Language Teaching. In theory, exploratory CALL provides the best of all worlds: learners are given simple procedures to follow that enable them to adapt the computer environment to their own needs and styles of learning. For example, learners can use, manipulate, and analyze language in an open-ended problem-solving and/or database-like environment (Higgins, 1988). By allowing unlimited access to a variety of information about and activities concerning the target language, the learner is encouraged to *explore*. It is, consequently, the genre of CALL software that is both richest in content and most closely aligned with a mediated approach promoting critical and creative thinking and realistic language use.

Clearly, there is no one "optimal" type of software for language learning. All of the software types reflected in Figure 6.1 can be used, and used well, when carefully incorporated into a balanced, eclectic curriculum. An eclectic approach to language teaching—one that combines a variety of activities—is certainly the rule of the day. Moreover, no one type of activity is considered "better" than others. It is a matter of mix, integration, and careful pacing that shapes the communicative classroom. The danger with computers is that too much time and trust may get invested into single types of activities at the expense of an eclectic mix or variety of on-line activity types. Sadly, the single type of task that prevails in both software design and, in turn, instructional use is the independent-study, system-user paradigm that usually focuses on drills. As we have learned over the last decades, drills, while an essential part of language teaching and learning, are of limited value. They need to be undertaken sparingly. The temptation with CALL is to have students do on-line drills at the expense of other activity—CALL is, after all, an efficient way to drill. However, there are, as we can see in Figure 6.1 and will see more of in Chapters 7 and 8, a number of ways to use the computer that extend well beyond that for which it is most commonly perceived as being useful for language education.

WHAT COMPUTERS CAN AND CAN'T "DO"

Today when we sit down in front of a computer, chances are there is a familiar graphical interface on the screen through which we make selections, answer questions, and navigate through the software applications we are using. By clicking, or dragging, or dropping the mouse on a given portion of the screen, we can affect the change or 'reaction' we desire. This change or reaction is represented on the screen so that we understand whether or not we have been successful. If, for example, I am exploring a "room" in a simulated environment—an adventure game in a haunted house—a click on the right-hand door's knob "opens" that door and allows me to guide myself (the graphical character on the screen) through that door. This interaction is much different from answering multiple choice questions described in the preceding section. Or is it?

In effect, underneath the fancy graphics, sound effects, and an input device (the mouse), the human-machine dialogue is essentially the same as the bare bones exchange described earlier. The contemporary version, by virtue of more sophisticated visuals and possibilities for screen manipulations, is certainly more comfortable and empowering than the *typing of text in the dark* of old. In the graphical environment, the system cues the user to make a choice, to do something, and responds according to what the user does. Again, this is what computers can be made to do easily and well. The fact that the way they do it is getting more attractive as processing power speeds up, does not change this elemental format for machine-user interaction: same dialogue, new interface.

To be thoughtful, critical consumers of instructional software products, we need to step back and consider what it is machines *can and can't do* to complement language learning processes.

Computers:

CAN	CAN'T[4]
Judge Answers: • Multiple Choice • Fill in the blanks	Judge unexpected input
Provide Feedback: • Correct/Incorrect • Remedial sequences • Suggestions and encouragement	Provide feedback beyond a predetermined, and therefore limited, list of messages
Record: • Learner's writing • Speech • Progress	Give feedback that addresses unexpected input; in other words, meaning
Provide Comparisons for self-check: • Text, pictures, audio segments, video • Spectographs	
Promote critical and creative thinking	Engage learner in rich negotiation of meaning characteristic of face-to-face interaction
Motivate Task Persistence	Motivate depth and quality of engagement characteristic of human interaction

CLT AND COMPUTERS

Looking at what computers *can* do, they potentially have an enormous amount to offer the learning process. There is, however, a danger in taking these *cans* too much to heart. The machine/software can potentially

---

[4] Over three centuries ago, Rene Descartes encapsulated the artificial intelligence argument by pointing out that a machine could never modify its output in response to meaning expressed through language as "even the most stupid men can do." There are contemporary scholars who believe that the needed computing power to achieve what "stupid men can do" is realizable (see, for example, Kurzweil, 2000).

provide these kinds of benefits, but, remember, it is the *learner* who makes up 51% of the conversation. It is she, after all, who must initiate the dialogue (the 1%), then engage equally in the response exchange scenario to keep the conversation going. The danger lies in losing sight of the learner's role when thinking about computer power. We have somehow come to be conditioned to think of the machine as *doing*, and the human as being *done to*, rather than being consistently aware of the human agency required for these machines to be in any way effective tools.

Note that in the CAN and CAN'Ts above, the shortcomings of computers are chiefly related to their limited capacity for dealing with language in a meaningful way. Machines cannot, and may never fully simulate the complexities of human language as it is used for Communication between individuals. The processing required to do so is inherently human and takes place within complex webs of social, physical, cognitive, and experiential factors that constitute communication. While CALL software can provide opportunity for some types of language learning activity, it falls short when it comes to realistic, communicative practice. This is particularly problematic as CLT places special emphasis on productive, meaningful use of language in all of its complexity. The following section examines the computer in an entirely different role from that described in the previous sections; that is, rather than being used by single learners for individualized practice, we'll look at the computer as a potential catalyst around which rich Communication practice can be orchestrated.

CRAFTING CONTEXTS OF USE

Unfortunately, machines are often perceived and used as a way to occupy students so the teacher can attend to other matters. This notion of 'freeing the teacher' has, in fact, been a powerful force behind software development and technology integration in education. With students *productively*[5] engaged with the machine, that thinking goes, the teacher can devote time and attention to individual learners. This is certainly a potential plus in the language classroom where one-on-one, task-oriented communication with a native speaker is a desirable feature of the learning process. However, the teacher can be just as freed, and more likely to be a

---

[5] Recall the manufacturing metaphor in Chapter 1.

motivated player in the learning activity if she has carefully constructed authentic tasks that require collaboration around, rather than individuation with, the machines.

As the example above illustrates, successful use of computers in language instruction tends to depend far less on hardware and software and more on the ways in which these get *used* in instructional contexts. plain-Jane, mediocre software can be used beautifully to meet instructional goals (e.g., a simple math drill where one learner looks at the screen and her partner does not while each asks and answers questions about what appears there). Likewise, slick, expensive "multimedia" software can be used disastrously (recall María). What makes or breaks good use is the *context* that teachers craft, orchestrate, and support with the computer.

The term *context* includes the many interrelated factors (e.g., learning goals, beliefs, shared experience, and the like) that go into computer use for language instruction. One of these factors is the *sociophysical* context of computer use. This is the physical and metaphorical space in which the computer resides in an instructional setting. That space—be it in the back, front, side, center, or closet of the classroom, or in a laboratory—speaks a great deal about how the machine and its role get perceived and, of course, how it ultimately gets used. The computer can consequently get cast as integral or marginal to the classroom society. If, for example, the machine is relegated to a 'private space'—a corner far from central activity—then subsequent activity with and around it will, for the most part, be perceived within the room's society as 'private.' As we saw with María, when the computer is located on the margins of the classroom, activity with it becomes 'marginal' in people's hearts and minds. In María's case, the computer became a kind of babysitter, taking care of an immediate problem for the teacher. To María, it became a kind of punishment, or 'timeout' away from the society she, like all children, wants to be a part of. However, if the computer is 'centralized' both physically and socially, then activity related to it will be perceived as shared and central to the social and academic workings of the class as a whole (e.g. Lilia's classroom). There are times, of course, when private work may be desirable. The risk is in overusing the machine as a sitter, tutor, reward or punishment. For language learning, private work is better done in contexts designed for private work, using a home computer for example, or working on an independent project in a computer laboratory. Language classrooms offer precious opportunities for guided use and meaningful interaction with language, not for isolation.

Pairing, Collaboration, and Off-Screen Talk

The previous sections provide explanation as to why a computer is not the ideal conversation partner in terms of practicing communicative skills. Present limitations prevent it from simulating the richness and complexity of face-to-face negotiation of meaning that is the hallmark of being human. Some continue to argue that, on the contrary, the machine's infinite patience and forgiving quality ("No, try again." *ad infinitum*) are complementary characteristics that meet the needs and goals of language learners. Others observe that, because there are rarely enough machines for students, pairing students is a practical necessity. Wouldn't it be nice if that pairing of learners had some payoff regarding communicative skills development?

Might the computer be cast into a role that encourages student-student interaction, thus overcoming the shortcomings of the computer as a means of communicative practice? Several studies have examined the type and quality of discourse that occurred between language learners when they were paired at computers. Close examination of paired learning sessions revealed that, left to their own devices, students engaged in very little conversation with each other while working around the computer. Moreover, what conversation students *did* engage in was "impoverished" as regards structural complexity and meaning. Apparently, as a "third party" in a conversation, the computer seems to do more to distract than to encourage student-student interaction (Meskill, 1993; Piper, 1986).

A particularly interesting aspect of these investigations is that machines were consistently situated in an "agentive" framework. Both the software and contexts for using it were designed as if the computer (and software) were "doing something" that would affect student-student interaction. But in fact, few software products are designed to prompt and sustain student interaction. The vast majority of products are designed with a single user in mind, not two. Consequently, frameworks for cueing and supporting off-screen talk are not inherently part of the stimulus. In addition, the socio-physical contexts in which these trials took place had the locus of the task residing with the computer, not external to it. In other words, the activity itself (working with a partner and one machine) was not configured within and as a part of the larger learning context. What students did with the machine had no consequence beyond what they had caused the computer to do at a given moment. These two aspects, single-user software design and decontextualized usage, possibly serve to constrain interaction between learners, rather than support it.

Since these early "clinical" examinations of off-screen talk between paired learners, three related initiatives have attempted to cast the computer in a role of a stimulus for student-student communication:

1) software design characteristics that prompt, support, and encourage motivated student-student exchanges are being developed and tried out (Meskill & Jiang, 1996);

2) native speaker software designed for "one-computer classrooms" has become a stimulus for paired ESL student exchange (for example, Meskill, 1992; Snyder & Palmer, 1986); and

3) teacher and contextual support (as we witnessed in Lilia's classroom) is becoming recognized, described, and systematized (Meskill & Jiang, 1996; Meskill, Mossop & Bates, 1999; Sasson, 1996).

There are three important considerations in orchestrating communicative activities around instructional software: software design, using native-speaker software, and crafting the contexts in which these get used.

Software Design

Explicit cues for paired student-student conversation can be built directly into software applications. For example, Jiang has developed a series of lessons for ESL students that employ visuals (paintings and photographs) that inspire individual interpretation. She incorporates these visuals in a software context that cues paired ESL learners to discuss, interpret, and use various modes of description while interacting with one another. In this instance, the computer directly cues interaction by stimulating student exchange through visuals and accompanying text prompts. She also includes guidance for these conversations by way of functional language they might use such as the structures and vocabulary of description, interpretation, and expressing opinions. In pilot trials, this open-ended, yet guided framework works well in stimulating and supporting off-screen talk.

Unfortunately, the vast majority of commercially available instructional software is designed for the single user. This means that the onus for orchestrating and promoting purposeful communication around this software is on the teacher. The section *Crafting Contexts of Use*, in this chapter, addresses this responsibility.

Native-speaker software

In addition to commercially produced language learning software, there are numerous products in the target language (native speaker software) that can stimulate motivated student-student interaction. Games and informational databases designed for content areas such as social studies, language arts, and science, for example, are products that can serve to stimulate and sustain very rich communicative activities when an instructor carefully crafts language learning activities around them. These native-speaker products tend to be rich in content and motivated use of real problem-solving discourse. Their designs are, after all, not preoccupied with Form. They are not focused on discrete language objectives, but on doing and thinking other things *using the target language*. Their emphasis is on real tasks that require language *use* rather than on automatic or metalinguistic knowledge that tend to be the focus of a good many CALL designs.

Point talk, an example...
In the following scenario, this group of ESL middle school learners is working on a simulation game – *SimCity*—in which they construct and manage a metropolitan area of their own design. During this complex process, they are required to keep track of a number of variables for their cities to run successfully. Here they are tracking crime and disasters using the target language, English, in conjunction with the concrete referents that appear on the computer screen:

Alfredo: [*reading from the screen*] Primary city is out of range.

Juan: Hey! This crime! [*points to crime indicator on screen*]

Teacher: You have no disasters yet?

Alfredo: [*looking at teacher*] Whey they have crime in my city?

Teacher: How could you have crime? Do you have any people? [*points to population indicator on screen*]

Alfredo: No. I don't know [*takes up mouse*] They have crime. Is says...then how far up am I? [*pointing with cursor to information box on screen*]

Juan: Oh gosh. Look a this. Look at this [*points to screen*] I still have way to go.

Teacher: How's yours, Nadine?

Nadine: I'm doing just fine. Right now I'm making a very big, large shopping mall. [*points to screen*]

These learners and their instructor are using "point talk," an example of the interplay between a medium's characteristics and the kind of language learning that can take place around computers. Learners and teachers point to and use what is on the screen to illustrate, support, and 'anchor' what it is they are hearing and saying to one another. The instructor's objective is for learners to use these items and structures productively while working on the computer and talking about what they are doing. Forms can be called attention to by pointing out representations on the screen—words, pictures, animations, video clips – as learners are productively making meaning in reference to the concrete referents they see on the screen.

A language instructor would be hard pressed to find a more lively, communication-focused activity that incorporated cross-curricular content and concepts while providing learner-controlled investment. These learners initially have worked away from the computer planning and practicing the words and ideas they would need. When they are finished working on the computer, the teacher will debrief on their city-building experiences to recycle and expand on those same forms, vocabulary items, and concepts.

SUMMARY

Like any instructional tool, computers can be used well to complement learning processes. When used to support second language acquisition, there are a number of roles for the machine that make sense given its unique constraining and supporting features. Understanding these features and the various manners of exploiting these, through the careful design of instructional activity, constitutes the difference between the experiences of María and Lilia described at the beginning of this chapter. In the case of María, limited understanding of both the needs and processes of the second language learner and the potential of the computer to support these led to instructional activity that may not have served the child well. On the other hand, Lilia's experience revealed some careful planning and implementation on the part of an instructor who had a sense of both the learner and the technology in consort. In short, designing and implementing computer-focused language learning is not unlike planning with other media and resources. It requires an eye to the special features of both the learner and the medium.

Activities

Activity 1: Grammar Highlights

The following learner activities require no prior knowledge of word processing, but assume some introductory work with parts of speech. Each activity's objective is threefold: task-based listening, parts of speech in the target language, and text-editing basics in the target language

This activity requires that students highlight (boldface, underline, shrink) different parts of speech in the sentences provided. They practice cursor movement, highlighting, text editing, and the language that accompanies it. This is a fun 'first time' word processing activity.

Note: Because of differing typing speeds and facility with a computer keyboard and the software, a lot of student-student talk will result as the class tries to perform the same tasks at different speeds. Listen to these conversations and encourage student-student involvement in the problem-solving process.

Prerequisites: some prior work labeling parts of speech

Lexis: cursor (up, down, right, left arrows), mouse, click, Enter key, SHIFT key, underline, boldface, shrink, edit, print

Set-up: Pairs of students at computers with Microsoft Word ready with new document on screen.

> Step 1) Tell the class they will be highlighting three basic parts of speech on the computer screen (You may want to briefly review *noun, verb, adjective.*)
>
> Step 2) Handout the following:
>
> > PARTS OF SPEECH
> >
> > A) A computer keyboard has more keys than a typewriter.
> >
> > B) With the mouse we can point, click, and select.
> >
> > C) A diskette is flat, rectangular, and plastic.
> >
> > SENTENCE A: <u>UNDERLINE</u> NOUNS.
> > SENTENCE B: **BOLDFACE** the VERBS.
> > SENTENCE C: SHRINK the ADJECTIVES.

Step 3) Have students type in the first sentence on the handout. This can be done with one partner dictating and the other typing. Circulate and check accuracy.

Step 4) As a group, decide which is the first noun to appear in the sentence.

Step 5) When the group has decided that "keyboard" is the first noun, tell them to move cursor to the "k" in the word keyboard and, using the mouse or touchpad, click, hold, and highlight the word.

Step 6) Have them locate the **U**nderline icon at the word processor's toolbar and click on it.

Step 7) Have them repeat the same procedure for the remaining nouns in Sentence A. Circulate and give assistance.

Step 8) For sentence B, have learners repeat steps 3-7 but instead of underlining nouns, **B**olding the verbs.

Step 9) For sentence C, have learners repeat steps 3-7 but instead of bolding the verbs, change the font size to a small one to shrink the adjectives.

Step 10) Students can print out their finished text and jot down any instructions/clarifications they may need to do more of the same in the future.

Expansion:

1) Dictation
Give the following dictation. Depending on the keyboarding skills of your group, you may first want to have learners use pencil and paper, then transfer the passage to the word processor.

> A printer is a useful and helpful machine. It prints out information from the computer which has been revised, checked, and edited. A printout of your text is called a hard copy. Often it is easier to read and edit a hard copy than the text on a computer screen. Which do you prefer?

Have learners underline the nouns, boldface the verbs, and shrink the adjectives.

2) Discussion
Discuss with the class some possible reasons for highlighting words they write.

3) Intonation
Take an existing dialogue or one that students have written and have pairs highlight words to show appropriate stress and intonation features.

EXAMPLE: You don't **want** to, **do** you?

Students can also transcribe native speaker speech and highlight patterns of stress and intonation as they hear these.

Variations
There are numerous possibilities for using the highlight (and colorizing and animating, as well) functions to draw learner attention to Form. Lessons around sounds, syntactic structures, or functions can also be developed using the word processor.

Activity 2: Carmen Sandiego

The "Carmen" series are interactive simulations that motivate learners to use reference materials to "win the game" (capture the perpetrator of a crime). For this sample activity, we'll use *Where in the World is Carmen Sandiego?* (social studies/geography) though any of the Carmen games can be used to great advantage. Currently they are published in English, Spanish, French, and Japanese.

Students play the role of detective. Their job is to identify, track down, and arrest an international criminal. The format requires that they look up key information (monetary systems, flags, capital cities) in an almanac while trying to catch the thief.

Carmen is rich in motivated communication possibilities. An added bonus of the *World* version is that language learners are also expanding their knowledge of other lands and cultures.

The Crime Matrix (game warm up)
Objective: Familiarize learners with detective work and its vocabulary.

Prerequisites: WH-question formation

Set-up: Classroom with learners facing blackboard.

Materials: one copy completed matrix
one copy dictation
students need paper and pencil

Step 1) Give students the following dictation (you can opt to have them write only the witness report if you wish).

Last night someone stole an expensive gold watch from _____ (local department store). A store clerk described what happened:

"A man in a black raincoat came into the store as we were closing. He reached into the glass showcase, took the watch, and walked out. I saw him get into a gray car. He was tall, had a medium build, and green eyes. His hair was blond and straight. He looked Scandinavian."

Step 2) As students are checking their work, draw the following matrix on the board omitting the names and information in the lower cells. Reread the passage as needed.

Step 3) Tell students they are detectives who have been assigned to solve the case of the missing gold watch. Four suspects, George

Jones, Zack Zimmerman, Sherman Shell, and Rick Roberts are in custody (note: have the class repeat these names after you to practice their pronunciation). To find out which is the criminal, they must match the description the witness gave to one of these four men.

Step 4) Give the completed matrix (below) to one student who will play the role of the file keeper. He or she should sit apart from the others. Tell the class that this person possesses all the necessary files for them to solve the crime. Their job is to ask him/her questions that will help them fill in the matrix and find the criminal.

Have another student come to the board and act as recorder – the one who writes the information in the appropriate boxes of the matrix as facts are discovered.

Suspect	Height	Weight	Eyes	Hair	Nationality	Car
George Jones	6' 1"	183	green	blond	Italian	burnt orange
Zack Zimmerman	6' "	186	green	red	Irish	tan
Sherman Shell	6' 2"	185	green	blond	Swedish	gray
Rick Roberts	6' 3"	182	green	black	Syrian	gray

Activity 3: Examining Software

Where we clearly need to be very critical consumers of all technologies, instructional software presents a particular challenge. Publishers and vendors have done a very good job of marketing these kinds of software. A common tactic is to put a "solution spin" on instructional software. This spin casts computer-based learning in the role of solution for a whole range of instructional "problems."
Here are some examples:

Individualized! Message—learners rarely get individualized attention in other instructional formats; learner better able to decide the route and processes of her learning than a teacher

Self-paced! Message—the learner is better off in an autonomous role whereby all decisions are made by her in her own time

Interactive! Message—interaction with a human instructor can be simulated and even improved upon on-line

Motivating! Message—the machine can induce in a learner an excitement for, and consequent persistence with learning

So prevalent and convincing are these pitches that we are often convinced there is a problem to which to apply the touted solution. Advertisements also play on the competitive dimension of education: *Prepare your students for a high tech world—other schools are, you'd better catch up! Don't be left behind!* Promises of higher achievement are common and naturally appeal to administrations who hold the purse strings for such purchases.

Team up with a partner and look closely at a language teaching software package or two. Here are some ideas of what to look for, but by no means should you limit yourselves to these foci.

Sample Software Review Sheet

Name of Program: _____ **Publisher/Year:** _____

Target Level/Learners: _____

Brief Description of Package, its objectives and instructional strategies:
_____
_____
_____
_____

Level of Challenge	low	medium	high
Ease of Use	low	medium	high
Motivation	low	medium	high
Feedback	low	medium	high
Learning	low	medium	high
Mileage	low	medium	high
Flexibility	low	medium	high

Ideas for use with ONE LEARNER (comment on the type and quality of interaction/learning when the program is used by one language learner):
_____
_____
_____

TWO LEARNERS:
_____
_____
_____

GROUP WORK:
_____
_____
_____

With a Partner: Develop an instructional scenario that demonstrates an effective use of software drill for a given population in a given instructional context. Detail the needs, goals, constraints and current status of language learning that indicate that computer-based drill is optimal at this point. Describe the drill software—both its content and format.

The Language of computer collaboration

> I'll do it.
> Let me.
> Let's try...
> How about...
> I think we should...
> That's right..
> That's wrong../ not it.
> Why don't you..

Phrases such as these can be explicitly taught, modeled, and reviewed whenever learners work together using computers. Try adding to the list.

APPENDIX—FOR MORE INFORMATION ON CALL:

Internet Sites

CALL: Computer Assisted Language Learning
http://www.vein.hu/~rohonyia/kut1.us.html
This is an excellent resource for those wishing to hear and contribute to discussion on language professionals' views and opinions concerning Computer Assisted Language Learning. Links to a number of relevant papers and conference proceedings are also available through this site.

National Clearinghouse on Bilingual Education
http://www.ncela.gwu.edu/
The National Clearinghouse for Bilingual Education (NCBE) website is designed to assist language teaching professionals, administrators, and researchers in the quest to provide the best instruction to culturally diverse students. The site provides bilingual education resources including online libraries with journals, bibliographies, reports, and abstracts. Funded by the U.S. Dept. of Education, this well organized site also offers information concerning technical assistance, classroom aids, scholarly articles, and lesson plans.

Journals

Language Learning and Technology Journal
http://llt.msu.edu/

Language Learning & Technology is a refereed journal that began publication in July 1997. The journal seeks to disseminate research to foreign and second language educators in the U.S. and around the world on issues related to technology and language education *Language Learning & Technology* is a fully-refereed journal with an editorial board of scholars in the fields of second language acquisition and computer-assisted language learning. The journal is published exclusively on the World Wide Web.

Computer Assisted Language Instruction Consortium (CALICO) Journal
http://www.calico.org
Southwest Texas State University
116 Centennial Hall
San Marcos, TX 78666
(812) 245-1417

CALICO, the Computer Assisted Language Instruction Consortium, is a professional organization that serves a membership involved in both language education and high technology. CALICO has an emphasis on modern language teaching and learning, but reaches out to all areas that employ the languages of the world to instruct and to learn. CALICO is a recognized international clearinghouse and leader in computer assisted learning and instruction. The *CALICO Journal* is a quarterly publication devoted to the exploration of the new technologies as applied to language learning. The oldest publication and professional organization dedicated to issues of technologies implementation for language instruction. This quarterly journal includes technology-related research articles, software and book reviews, reviews of related conferences, and commentary.

Computer Assisted Language Learning
http://sun.swets.nl/sps/journals/call.html
Swets & Zeitlinger Publishers
P.O. Box 613
Royerford, PA 19468
(800) 447-9387

An international journal published quarterly by Swets & Zeitlinger Publishers. *Computer Assisted Language Learning* is an international journal dedicated to all matters associated with the use of computers in language learning. It provides a forum to discussions on discoveries in the field and the exchange of experience and information about existing techniques. The journal is wide-ranging and embraces a multitude of disciplines. Example areas of inquiry include: pedagogical principles and their application, observations and evaluation of CALL software, the application of artificial intelligence to language teaching, computer-assisted translation, multilingual learning systems, and computer-based learning environments. The audience for the journal is teachers and researchers, linguists, computer scientists, psychologists, and education professionals.

For further reading:

Bush, M. (1997). (Ed.). *Technology-Enhanced language learning.* Chicago: National Textbook Publishing.
Cameron, K. (1999) *CALL: Media, design & applications.* The Netherlands: Swets & Zeitlinger.
Egbert, J. and Hanson-Smith, E. (1999) *CALL environments.* Washington, DC: TESOL International Publications.
Levy, M. (1997). *Computer-assisted language learning: Context and conceptualization.* New York: Oxford University Press. (212) 679-7300
Pennington, M. (1996). (Ed.) *The power of CALL.* Houston: Athelstan Publishers.
Sperling, D. (1998). (2nd Ed.). *Dave Sperlings's Internet guide.* Upper Saddle River, NJ: Prentice Hall. (800) 428-5331

CALL IS Software List

TESOL
1600 Cameron St., Suite 300
Alexandria, VA 22314

This yearly publication of the TESOL CALL Special Interest Section includes descriptions and reviews by practicing ESL teachers.

7. Computer Communication Tools

Out of chaos the imagination frames a thing of beauty.

John Lowes
Road to Xanadu

At an adult basic education program in a large urban area, an ESL teacher initiates a newly arrived Vietnamese gentleman, Thông, to a chat site established by the program. The purpose of the site is to link up non-native speakers of English with community members for online conversation. In a matter of a few days, Thông has befriended a member of the community through a number of e-mail exchanges. The native speaker with whom he communicates, Tom, corrects and elaborates on Thông's messages as a casual online tutor. Two weeks into their online friendship, they begin to seriously discuss the Viet Nam War and their respective experiences in it. As it turns out, Tom and Thông are both veterans of the War and one-time enemies. Through a series of difficult, heart-felt exchanges they jointly work through their respective experiences and together make sense of a senseless tragedy. By the fourth week, Tom has invited Thông and his family to his home for dinner. Their relationship ripens.

Across the river, a Business major at a large private university, Jerry, consults her online Japanese grammar reference as she composes a message to her project partner in Tokyo, an undergraduate Economics major. Their assignment is to co-construct a website that contains investor resources and utilities. They initially 'met' during a two-way video/audio session at the beginning of the semester, but have since forged their partnership in the project through online exchanges within the site they are constructing. Thus far, they have managed to co-design the look and feel of the site, and are now negotiating what investor tools will be included, how these will work, and how the remaining work will be undertaken. Jerry cc's her Business Investing professor and her Japanese professor who will award her a composite grade based on the language and business concepts instantiated in the process and product of her collaborative project. All of these negotiations take place in Japanese, Jerry's second language as of three semesters.

At a middle school in a local suburb, two beginning learners of French are sitting in the school library at a computer. They are working on composing a simple "day in the life" description of their day, in French. Their teacher will work with them to polish the final version of their composition that they will then mail to their sister school in Benin, Africa. Their sister class will in turn send descriptions of their daily lives, written in English, back to the U.S. children. As they compose, they are quick to refer to what they are constructing on the screen by pointing and discussing the content and structure of their multimodal text. They co-construct, co-edit, and co-create using as much French as they have so far learned and the new vocabulary and structures they are motivated to locate and incorporate via online references.

These scenarios represent a minute smattering of instances whereby language educators are making powerful use of telecommunications in their language teaching. All over the globe, such projects and activities are blooming. Motivating such implementations is the centrality of Communication in the language acquisition process. The computer provides opportunities to communicate both through it, by typing in and receiving messages; with it, by composing written work to be read online and off; and around it by stimulating and supporting Form- and Communication- focused talk in the process.

COMPUTERS AND WRITING

Computers are exquisite tools for writing, for facilitating communication through the written word. In fact, it is not surprising that word processing has done more to alter the way humans think and write than any other literacy innovation (Murray, 1995; Tyner, 1998). Moreover, word processing technology appeared on the scene at a most propitious time in history—a time when the focus of writing instruction, and instruction in general, shifted from a product-oriented approach to a process-oriented philosophy. This process-oriented tool showed up just in time to complement the messy, complex, non-linear activity of composing thought.

Indeed, word processing is not just the processing of *words*, it is the processing of *ideas*, which is the central activity of composing written communications. When considering second language composing, the revision capabilities of word processors are a huge boon not only to the process of composing but also to developing a feel for how the language operates. It is an extraordinary opportunity for second language learners to become intimate with the language they are learning to read and write. Also, in terms of Affect, word processing represents an opportunity for second language learners to produce a neat, well-written, well-edited version for others to read, thus instilling a sense of audience and pride in what they wish to communicate.

Especially potent for language learners is the fact that face-to-face communication is the most challenging aspect of mastering and using an additional language. What gets said and understood happens too quickly to be subjected to any thoughtful editing along the way.

Telecommunicating asynchronously allows review, reflection, and revision.

Built in to just about any form of electronic exchange—communications via computer from one writer to another—is the facility to compose (meaning to edit to your heart's content) your message at your own pace, in your own time, with whatever resources you deem necessary. Even in synchronous, two-way online conversations, if you feel the need to take extra time to think and compose, it is perfectly appropriate to signal this to your interlocutors—something that is often awkward for language learners in live, face-to-face communications.

In electronic communications there tends to be less focus on "composition" in the traditional sense of logic, coherence, and rhetorical norms. Rather, electronic communications is breeding its own, novel form of communication that by definition lies somewhere between what is truly "writing" and what is truly "speaking." It is neither and both at the same time.

> **Note**: In order to record thoughts as quickly as possible (an essential component in the writing process), keyboarding skills are absolutely necessary. Hunting and pecking can hamper more than enhance the recording of thoughts in progress. For language students who have poor keyboarding skills, two strategies seem to work—either build language learning lessons and tasks around the teaching of touch typing, or assign learners to independently improve their finger positioning and work on increasing their speed using a typing tutor program. (See the *Activities* section at the end of this chapter.)

Asynchronous Written Communication

The term *asynchronous* means "not in real time." When you write asynchronously, you anticipate that your text will be read when you have decided it is ready to be read. This is the case whether you click on the print icon or the send button. You will also be aware that what you write can not only be read, but *re*read. As such, unlike most of oral communication, it is open to critique. Whether the computer is used to compose messages intended to be read in a telecommunications environment (e.g. e-mails, blogs, social networking venues, etc.) or compositions (longer stretches of discourse that adhere to traditional forms of rhetoric and style and are fashioned as "print" rather than telecommunications texts) they fall under the category of *asynchronous communication*. Both types of writing are *composed* in the sense that they are revisited, edited, and fashioned with some 'print-like' intent. In both cases, the delay between the act of writing and a reader's reading of these writings is the purview of the writer—it is her decision as to when a document is "done" and ready to be read.

Composition as Communication

Composition here refers to composing in the traditional sense, that is, writing to be *read* in the traditional sense of reading ink, not screens. With very few exceptions, word processing is the tool of choice for contemporary writers. The technology clearly meets the criteria for a useful thinking tool in that it enables writers to mindfully attend to more complex mental tasks by facilitating or performing simpler, time consuming tasks for them. For teachers too, the fact that students now submit neat, readable, high quality written work is a boon. Neat, readable final products also mean that students' writings can be shared, even published, increasing a learner's sense of readership that extends beyond the teacher. Electronically created compositions, moreover, means that teachers can add notes, commentary, questions, and suggestions directly to a student's draft. It also implies that writing portfolios can be designed to show drafts with changes highlighted. This affords the teacher a clear-cut view of a learner's progress in composing skills.

The opportunity to undertake painless revisions makes word processing an optimal tool for the composing process. It is, after all, widely accepted that the majority of what good writers do, what comprises the most thought and effort on the part of the writer, is the revision/editing process. Additionally, for writers in a second language, this process is potentially charged with rich opportunities for thought, communication, and developing awareness of target language forms and norms. Word processed drafts can be used in peer conferencing and conferencing with the teacher. Because it is both readable and malleable, the document in progress is fully open to input, critique, and discussion both in terms of form and content, and meaning.

Composing Asynchronous Messages

The history of human activity as regards asynchronous written communications is rich and lengthy. It is also much longer than our relatively short-term love affair with telecommunicating. For centuries people have composed messages—love missives, business communiqués, threats, warnings, propositions—all physically transported to an intended reader. The time span within which these deliveries were completed was sometimes predictable (she lives across town and reads her three o'clock mail over tea) and many times not (the potentially sixteen hands that will carry a message from Paris to Siberia). The etiquette and protocols for hand-carried written communications had a long period of time in which to evolve and a series of sociocultural climes in which to accommodate norms of practice. For example, the system of communicating one's state of mind by the type, arrangement, and color of the flowers accompanying a hand-carried missive was not unlike present-day choices of font, images, arrangement, and color of the texts we send through the ether.

Our furiously fast, condensed, yet terribly brief history of online communication has been more of a free-for-all in terms of rules and acceptabilities. An "anything goes" atmosphere continues to prevail in spite of numerous attempts from all corners of society to formalize the laws of "netiquette" (see the end of this chapter for some sample attempts). For language instruction, this open frontier of communications represents both "the best of" and "the worst of" for teaching and learning. On the one hand, students have an opportunity to compose and receive messages written in the target language in a more or less 'free form' manner. Some have even praised this capacity for free form communication as resembling the spontaneous negotiation of meaning characteristic of live interaction, an activity considered by many as central to the second language acquisition process. On the other hand, free-formedness in text does not model what traditional print is all about. For the majority of its quotidien purposes, it is characterized by strict form and convention. The idiosyncratic shorthand characteristic of the bulk of electronic messages is not, in other words, the best model of target language writing OR speaking for non-native speakers to emulate. This "somewhere in betweenness" can be confusing and should be handled carefully in instructional contexts. Learners must be continually reminded that where we once had two facets of the new language to learn – the spoken form and the written form – we now have a third – the 'e-text form.'

TELECOMMUNICATING AS A SECOND LANGUAGE

At present, you can write to anyone on the planet in just about any language you choose. There are far too many excellent examples of ways language professionals have made use of this simple technology for teaching and reinforcing language learning to include here. From highly structured to more open-ended communicative tasks and assignments, the medium has served to get language learners using the language productively through communication with others. To implement new, or to extend existing online practices, here are some considerations that can help you in developing relevant tasks, their parameters, and forms of assessment.

Goals/task development

Like face-to-face interaction, predicting the precise processes and outcomes of human communication online is not easy. However, without some planning that considers the needs and goals of a specific group of students, your immediate and long-term instructional goals, and a certain range of potentialities concerning what task-based communication might look like, online communication may be as much of a free-for-all as putting your students in small groups and telling them to "talk." This is not to say that completely unstructured chatting is not valuable, it is. And it is activity that can benefit students a great deal if they are motivated, employ effective language learning strategies in the process, and have similar opportunities outside of class time. Unstructured online communication has the added benefits of:

1) being recorded; a record of unstructured talk can be used as the focus of linguistic, sociolinguistic analysis, etc. (**Form**);

2) allowing for meaning to take precedence over form; (**Communication**);

3) providing a forum for the nascent L2 voice to develop (**Affect**); and

4) if a partner is a more capable peer or native speaker, meaning-based feedback that will lead a student to attend to the manner in which her messages are constructed (**Communication** with attention to **Form** with positive **Affect**).

Constructing tasks that require your students to communicate online entails much the same kind of thinking as task design with the other media and technologies discussed thus far. The crucial elements are that learners have a stake in communicating, and that the task undertaken carries some consequence for the class as a whole. The stake in communicating must be such that students become aware of how the target language works. The task they undertake online must result in something useful, even critical, being brought back to the class. One of the most frequently used tasks that fit these criteria is the pen pal/biography assignment. The learner interviews a native speaker online, elicits and collects specific information about that pen pal, and presents the person in some kind of biographical form to the rest of the class—all using the target language. The language of personal information and interview are the linguistic focus for data gathering, and the language of description for the report-back portion of the assignment. I have known teachers who have had their language students submit not only a formally composed biography of their online partner, but a record (printout and digital copy) of the semester's worth of conversing. She uses that record to assess how and what language has become more complex and exact as a result, at least in part, to these exchanges.

Telecommunications represents an excellent, relevant forum to teach what we think of as standard forms of address, organized by degree of formality. Just as learners need to be familiar with the different ways we speak depending on context, they likewise need to know and apply this understanding in online contexts. It may be that you assign learners, or they write independently to strangers for business purposes. Regardless, tone truly counts. We tend to forget this as the medium acquires an informal and chatty tenor. However, just as in face-to-face interaction, the relative power status between interlocutors must be detected and respected, and an appropriate register employed.

Social Networking

In addition to individuals exchanging messages, another form of asynchronous telecommunications has become an effective tool type for language teaching and learning is *social networking*. Social networking differs from simple e-mail or text messaging in that a number of people can read what an individual writes, post a response, and have anyone (or a restricted set of people) respond. In earlier days, this kind of social networking was done through something called a bulletin board—an analogy that is useful in conceptualizing conferencing—its purposes and processes. Nowadays, we use venues such as blogs, Facebook or Twitter. Again, this happens mostly asynchronously, which carries implications for how these messages in general and the conference in particular are treated. Because a social networking participant can take as long as she wishes, or feels she needs, to fashion her contribution, there is a great deal of potential for balanced attention to form and meaning. Consequently, there is an opportunity for constructive, language-oriented tasks with the instructor and/or more capable speakers of the target language moderating and mediating task processes.

With specially constructed online instructional spaces, initiation of a discourse topic is typically the purview of the course instructor, but most social networking allows any registered participant to initiate a topic or thread for discussion. The rules for initiating and responding tend to emerge and evolve much as they do in live social situations. Indeed, an interesting social aspect of telecommunications is that the *rules* for conducting these sorts of conversations are "in progress." Becoming well-versed in the various styles and registers of target language speaking and writing is especially realizable in electronic communications. Whereas online groups tend to use a hybrid of norms borrowed from both the spoken and written media, they also develop their own idiosyncratic codes and conventions. Attending to forms, both standard and evolving, is an important aspect of using electronic communications with language learners. It is at once an excellent forum to draw attention to various registers and conventions, and one where atypical forms need to be labeled as such to save confusion for learners in the process of discovering how the target language works.

One interesting example of this evolution is the case of non-native speakers of English telecommunicating with native speakers. As part of their intensive, low-intermediate ESL course our University's Intensive English Language Program (IELP), students exchanged mail with native speaker pen pals—my TESOL graduate students, whose assignment was to provide informal language tutorial in the context of weekly conversational exchanges. The ESL students' assignment was to get to know the native speaker well enough to compose a biographical sketch of their pen pal and present this to the class. Two conventions particular to this situation are notable. First, ESL students' e-mail messages consistently began with an apology and an excuse. The apology deals with what they saw as "tardiness" in responding. Considering this was their first experience with the medium, their sense of an appropriate time lag was unformed. The excuse portion of the message typically contains either a "very busy" or "no access to machine" excuse in regards to tardiness.

> *I feel sorry for not answering your letter. I was absent in my computer class for 3 weeks, but I know this can't be a good excuse.*

The second curious convention that evolved in these exchanges is that the native speaker messages consistently ignored the apology. It is simply not acknowledged and, perhaps consequently, in many instances, fades from the non-native speakers' messages as time goes on. An additional salient convention is that, as in face-to-face interaction, the native speaker does a good deal of the topic initiation and topic control. She seems to ask more questions and shift topics more frequently than does the non-native speaker, at least initially. As time progresses, the non-native speaker seems to pick up this pattern of questioning and shifting topics to what interests her. Unlike face-to-face interaction, the non-native speaker has the luxury of time and online resources to compose questions and comments of personal relevance.

One of the best uses of telecommunications is as a forum to continue activity and discussions that occurred in class. Conversations can be reflected on and developed further through students' contributions to threaded online discussions once class is over. It can also serve as an excellent forum for students to submit written assignments; that is, students can post their assignments on the newsgroup thereby extending their audience from just the instructor to the entire class. Students can benefit from reading and commenting on one another's work and from the instructor's comments and corrections. Through this medium, assignments become public documents with potentially larger readerships and participation. This format is commonly referred to as blended learning.

Pairing and grouping learners to communicate electronically over a period of time where they take on specific tasks (exchange family recipes, describe objects in their home, etc.) and/or personae (a fictional character of their own design, a character from a familiar reading or television show) can serve to provide extra opportunity for learners to practice in an enjoyable manner. It can also provide a way for you to evaluate what they do outside of class if they submit the archives of their conversations at the end of their project. Not only can pairs and small groups be assigned regular communication, they can also be charged to co-build informational/entertainment websites with others. Such a co-building task can be structured to focus on particular language forms, lexis, or functions as needed.

SYNCHRONOUS WRITTEN COMMUNICATION

Synchronous communication via computer is the nearly instantaneous delivery of one writer's message to another, a process that more closely approximates real time communication than the asynchronous communications scenarios above. There are certainly some benefits that can be derived from "real time" communications as opposed to those that are delayed by correspondents reading and responding to messages at their leisure. When synchronous communications are coordinated—participants are logged on at the same time—the issue of whether the communication is more like "talk" or "text" is more acute. A great deal of research activity is being applied to study transcripts of these different forms of communication in an effort to characterize this uniqueness (see for example, Thorne, 1999). What we do know thus far is that the language of synchronous telecommunications is syntactically and lexically streamlined. There is an economy of words (abbreviations are frequent), and a simplification of forms (sentences are shorter and syntactically simple).

The constraints of synchronous electronic communication are obvious. As in face-to-face interaction, in order for exchange to occur, the person with whom you wish to communicate must be available and willing to do so, and be in a physical context where she *can* do so. If these conditions represent large obstacles, they're minor compared to the constraints on the discourse when one cannot see or hear an interlocutor while "talking" in real time. Without these kinds of paralinguistic information, one is left to interpret words on the screen. As mentioned earlier, in some respects this may simplify communication exchanges for language learners reading and writing messages in the target language. On the other hand, the lack of paralinguistic cues can limit and even detract from understanding. Research on utilizing text-based SCMC reveal more word truncations and acronyms (i.e., *u* for *you* ,*lol* for *lots of laughs*, etc.) reduced capitalization, by participants in order to maintain the flow and increase the speed of conversation by reducing the number of key strokes (Al-sa'di & Hamden, 2005). As these abbreviations and acronyms are not universal, teachers should set guidelines for students to follow when integrating text-based SCMC activities into their lessons. Additionally, this form of communication tended to result in less complex sentences. While this may appear a limitation, it potentially increases communication – a goal of any language learning activity. If the goal of using text-based SCMC is to improve student writing, these limitations also need to be accounted for.

SCMC platforms are excellent venues where learners of all ages can engage in both authentic communicative activities and instructional activities including listening, spoken communication, pronunciation practice, and writing. Despite constraints of SCMC, benefits include the following:

- increased reciprocity between participants
- encouragement of active learning
- increased contact
- prompt feedback

(Finkelstein, 2006)

SCMC can include activities where pairs and groups of students can meet both with and without the instructor. SCMC can be used for online tutoring with the instructor providing real time assessment. Streaming audio, video and text can result in rich tutorial sessions. Lesson targeting specific linguistic skills can be conducted. The streaming video can allow teachers to informally diagnose student comprehension because of being able to literally see the student. Misunderstandings in spoken communication can be remediated through the use of textual communication, and vocabulary or concepts can be more easily demonstrating by the teacher searching the Internet for appropriate graphics and video and sending links via text message. In essence,

SCMC can serve as a multimodal tool to assist in acquisition of the target language.

LABS

Computer-mediated communication between and among students can take place in any networked facility that uses conferencing software. This type of arrangement is called a Local Area Network, or LAN. Many businesses, colleges, and schools have installed these configurations so that joint conferencing can take place in real time. In language education, such set-ups are used most frequently for group writing and composing. Cues, questions, or heuristics are provided by a leader or instructor. Participants use these to respond, brainstorm, share ideas, and construct their own compositions. Responses to these stimuli can be instantaneously shared with all other students on the network who can in turn respond in real time. Though this process oftentimes appears chaotic, the kinds of language, thinking, and writing are quite lively and stimulating. There is ongoing, active, social construction of knowledge. Opportunities to exercise one's developing L2 voice abound.

For non-native speakers of the target language, the activity can be both challenging and cathartic. Unlike real time communication, there is far less risk of losing face. There is, moreover, a permissible lag time during which language learners can think, compose, and edit their messages. The quasi-anonymity of the enterprise (you have the option of using your real name or a pseudonym attached to your messages), compounded by the fact that there is more *time* to respond, and no one's face to respond to, can open up learners' voices in powerful ways. For example, while working with a group of TESOL graduate students in one of these facilities, a young Asian woman, who had said little in class up to that point, shared the following while the class corresponded on the LAN:

I'm cold and hungry and very, very lonely.

Her classmates tactfully responded in a variety of supportive ways, offering to share snacks, their sweaters, and inviting her to the movies.

Another example comes from a teacher of Japanese who frequently has her American undergraduates use this kind of set up to practice communicating in the target language. After viewing a very disturbing documentary about forced prostitution in Japan during World War II, a film about which she felt confident her students would have much to say, the students were mute. When they got to the LAN classroom, however, they opened up and shared their responses online readily and articulately.

In addition to the very often positive affective quality of these kinds of exchanges is the linguistic benefit of:

1) having the extra time to think, compose, and edit;
2) being able to reread, revisit, and reflect on what others have to say;
3) working with a variety of language types and forms that are both authentic and archived for close study.

Moreover, empirical evidence suggests that online 'utterances' are more syntactically and lexically complex than in face-to-face interactions (Warschauer, 1999). Students' final written products are superior to compositions composed offline, and the amount of peer and teacher input and feedback is much more than in traditional settings (Braine, 1997). Many instructors report using the record of these online conversations as a means of assessing students' strengths and weaknesses and plan subsequent instruction accordingly. Some even use printouts of online class discussion as the primary material for subsequent classes (see Warschauer & Meskill, 2000).

Beyond the classroom: Virtual Worlds

There are numerous opportunities for language students to practice the target language in synchronous exchanges with others via the Internet. Chat rooms, which resemble LAN interchanges in that each "room" is designed by a special topic/interest to be discussed, are real time communication sites. Anyone with an interest in the stated topic can 'enter' the room, assume her own or a fictitious identity, and participate. MOOs (Multi-user Object-Oriented environments) and MUDs (Multi-User Dimensions) are basically chat rooms with some special features. MUDs use text descriptions through which users envision themselves in (sometimes wildly) fictitious environments. MOOs use a combination of text and graphics to simulate three-dimensional, real time 'virtual realities' in which participants can interact. For example, there are numerous 'virtual' universities and other analogous spaces that have offices, common spaces, and classrooms that you can visually enter and in which you can interact with others visiting the same space. The tools participants can use in accessing expertise, playing available games, solving problems, making discoveries, and generally socializing with others in the same 'rooms' are the messages they write plus conventionalized symbols, abbreviations, and other forms of shorthand to express emotions/non-verbal signals. Second Life is a fascinating example of such a virtual world.

In terms of learning another language, a positive feature of these sites is the highly active, interactive, spontaneous nature of the communication going on. By eavesdropping, or 'lurking,' one can gain a sense of how language works in a very specific environment. In this way learners can increase their sociolinguistic, metalinguistic awareness of yet another form of communication in the target language.

DISTANCE LEARNING

Distance learning, formal instruction that occurs at a distance from others, has been around in various forms for decades. The best known historical manifestation of distance learning is the "correspondence course" that takes place via the postal system. Materials including texts, tapes, and tests are delivered by the Post Office to your home. When taking a correspondence course, completed assignments and tests are mailed to an instructor/grader. The Public Broadcasting Service (PBS) and some cable TV stations continue to offer similar services. You can complete courses—high school, GED, and college credit bearing—by watching instructional broadcasts and completing written assignments that are mailed in for assessment.

Attempts to deliver non-credit bearing, "enrichment" language learning opportunities have been similarly undertaken. For example, the popular language teaching television shows, *French in Action* and *Destinos,* can be viewed in conjunction with workbooks and other accompanying materials available through PBS. Programming in other world languages is frequently broadcast on local stations and is often freely accessible on the internet. The basic premise of these materials-supported language learning experiences is that the materials and approach are sufficiently motivating to keep independent learners engaged and learning the language on their own. As discussed in Chapter 2, there are learners who can and do make effective use of what they see on video/TV to improve their second language abilities. There are also, as discussed in Chapter 3, the great majority of us who need ongoing human contact, guidance, and support if we are to be successful learning another language.

Newer forms of distance learning are evolving all the time. Currently, you can register for entire language courses taught both asynchronously and synchronously via the Internet. What makes these telecommunications-based courses particularly unique and potentially powerful for the "at a distance learner" is the facility to correspond with a number of people—instructors, native speakers, and others—in the process of learning the language you are studying. A distance learning course delivered by computer can additionally contain all of the features of multimedia language learning (see Chapter 8). The reason it is discussed here, in a chapter on telecommunications, is that I believe it is the telecommunications aspect that makes this form of learning potentially more useful than the traditional 'study-the-workbook-listen-to-the-tapes-and-take-a-test' forms of distance learning.

In its most rudimentary form, a web-based distance learning course looks like an outline or menu of topics and activities that learners can opt to click on. In effect, what one sees and interacts with does not differ from a computer software program that provides options for instruction, access to content, and activities. What marks web-based courses is the communications facilities these possess. Not only are there spaces in which one can pose questions, make comments, and start up discussion threads, but there is the facility to post and share documents, links, and other media with others. The manner in which the instructor for such a course conceives of and implements the spaces, tasks, and assignments within these environments is a matter of pedagogical orientation, goals for a particular learner population, and creative thinking. Like the other media and technologies discussed thus far, the chunquing tool can again be employed to great advantage in devising activities that focus on both Form and meaning-based interaction.

The authoring tools available to instructors who wish to design online courses are many, varied, and easy to use. Your best approach is to find out what software your institution uses and supports and seek training in that package. Here are some basic techniques to start thinking about how to set up and guide learner communications within these environments.

Threaded Discussions
These are identical to discussion threads within other telecommunications venues in that a directory or menu of contributions under specific topic headings is built as discussion threads evolve. This is an excellent forum for learners to experience and practice cohesion, relevancy, and register. On-topic/off-topic guidance—scaffolding with cohesive devises to help readers and writers maintain topic threads in their contributions—uses language that is appropriate in register within various group discussion contexts. Learners self-monitor and edit their written contributions.

Talking Off
Distance Learning course environments can include just about any kind of information about which learners can communicate such as Internet websites, documents, images, audio sequences, etc. Talk and tasks can be orchestrated using any of these as stimuli.

Talking Around
Course environments can be designed to allow students to assemble their own materials around which they can build presentations, or use as supporting material to represent and defend their positions.

Self-test Tools
Rudimentary drill/test routines can be par of course design as well. These can be used as standard interactive drill exercises – fill in the blank (cloze), multiple choice, and true/false. Providing learners the opportunity to self assess is a critical part of any learning process. It is particularly fundamental to learning an additional language where an ongoing sense of progress is essential to maintain the much needed motivation for the complex undertaking that it is.

A strategy to enhance self-test features is to set up such tasks to be done in pairs. In this way, learners experience the extra benefit of using the target language to negotiate solutions to problems in the exercises. You can also enhance such activities by using interesting, extended passages, podcasts, and videos that are relevant to and inclusive of learners' lives and interests.

Pronunciation Work
Sound and video clips can be incorporated to model and train target language pronunciation. Assessment of learners' progress in pronunciation can also be evaluated by learner submission of self-produced audio and video files. Segment by segment feedback on the archived samples can be provided visually through text or mark up commentary, or aurally through instructor annotations. Tutorial coaching can also take place between the native and non-native speaker via two-way video conferencing.

Dyad Work/Small Group Work
Assigning pairs and small groups to work online together both synchronously and asynchronously is in many respects more straightforward than in a live classroom. Subtract the physical disruption of movement and clarification of roles and tasks, and the process can be seen as streamlined. Granted, any incidental linguistic benefit from the chaos that accompanies live grouping is lost. However, that digitally archived record of learners strategizing and negotiating may be of more or equal value.

NOTE: See the *Appendix* at the end of this chapter for a list of both synchronous and asynchronous tools available.

SOME SOCIOCULTURAL CONSEQUENCES OF ONLINE LEARNING

I'd like to share a snapshot of an asynchronous online course that I've taught for many years. It is among my personal favorites as it combines and explores my favorite intersections between Language, Literacy, and Technology (the title of the course). Here are some observations concerning the unique microsocietal and discourse trends I see evolving in this and other online courses, their implications for teaching and learning generally, and language learning in particular.

The course is designed for graduate students completing either a masters or doctorate in education. We explore a range of issues germane to teachers and researchers across content areas in terms of the changes in language and literacy electronic learning is inspiring. The central issues entertained throughout the course concern the roles electronic texts are playing in the development of contemporary readers and writers, how electronic texts differ from print, and how these differences influence language and literacy development in the native, second, and foreign languages. Students in this course typically represent a range of interests and content area specializations. They are not all from the same geographical areas. They are not all primarily language in education students. This makes the discussions and cross-fertilizations very rich.

To this online educator's way of thinking, the number one, key affordance of web-based instruction is the opportunity for rich, achievable discussions (see chart below). By maintaining the stance that knowledge and understandings best evolve through active, collaborative communication—questions, assignments, investment, and active participation—online instructional tasks emerge. Likewise, through the chunquing process, forms of learner online activity can take shape.

---

1) major asset = communication/community

2) instructor's social presence/connectivity = motivation

3) discussion parameters = guided/constrained by conversation maxims

4) enforcement of guidelines for acceptable participation/work = peer policing

5) archives for assessment = available to all (expanded readership/audience)

> 6) written communication = voice for the traditionally silenced

Formulae for the design of asynchronous web-based courses

A great deal of research points to the critical aspect of instructor "presence" as a predictor for successful learning and participation (Gunawardena & Zittle, 1997). Simply put, students sense investment on the part of the instructor through the quality and frequency of the cues, feedback, and responses she provides. Students in my online course have often expressed their positive response to my "presence" as a form of reassurance that what they are doing in the course is 'correct.' Although feedback from fellow students is highly prized as well, like in a live classroom, instructor comments ("presence") tend to add a sense of investment to student work.

A technique I have used that could be adapted for an online course in any content area, but that is particularly relevant for language-related courses, is the setting down of strict guidelines for online conversations. The central set of 'rules' is Howard Grice's *Conversational Maxims* (Grice, 1975):

> **Grice's Maxims**
>
> *QUANTITY*: make your contributions as informative as possible, but not more, or less, than is required.
>
> *QUALITY*: do not say that which you believe to be false or for which you lack evidence.
>
> *RELATION*: be relevant.
>
> *MANNER*: avoid ambiguity and obscurity, be clear, brief, and orderly.

Students can be alerted to and encouraged to discuss these simple rules for successful (what Grice calls "felicitous") conversation at the start of a course and then be pointed back to any one or all of them as needed during the course. That is, when students bend or break these rules they can be 'linked' back to them for review and remediation.

Another rule that helps to maintain coherence and order to online discussion is the 'edit before you send' rule. This prevents sloppy and/or ambiguous postings and helps learners tune their attention to the Form of their contributions as well as the messages they wish to convey. Both of these tactics – pointers to Grice's maxims and reminders of the *edit-before-send* rule – are tactics that could be used in the live classroom. These rules can be visually or aurally reinforced at any time. But the positive affordance of an online format is that learners do not lose face with these gentle reminders. Additionally with some careful orchestration, you, the instructor, can affect 'peer policing' whereby students monitor and remind one another of such rules. Focal rules can also shift from week to week: one week subject-verb agreement is highlighted – a paradigm highlighted and referred to and peer monitoring encouraged – and the next week the use of articles.

What I call the *archive/assessment/audience affordance* is the capacity to greatly expand students' audience. Rather than construct responses and messages solely for the purpose of teacher assessment, as is typical of the bulk of language classroom activity, learners read and respond as a community. A range of voices and opinions are thus heard and responded to. Assessments are ongoing and to a large degree become *self*-assessments as learners adhere to the edit-before-you-send rule.

The archival aspect is also quite powerful in terms of assessing an individual learner's performance for the course (e.g., assigning a grade). Not only do you have their written work (discussion records, collaborative scripts around tasks, and formal assignments), but you also have the reactions, responses, and assessments made by peers to these contributions. This input can greatly enrich the assessment process as it is no longer a matter of an instructor's judgment alone, but the composite of the learning community as a whole that matters. As such, throughout the course each student generates an automatic electronic portfolio of their work, that is, a record of their participation and assessments of their work by others.

Finally, I have found that asynchronous web-based learning environments are powerful voice-finding tools for those who are traditionally silenced in mainstream schooling venues. Women, minorities, and non-native speakers of English (the language in which the courses are taught and conducted) repeatedly praise the medium for allowing them a role, a place in the instructional process, unlike any they've ever had in a live classroom. They also express, in very articulate ways, critical issues from unique, heretofore silenced, perspectives. For language instruction, this is a particularly exciting aspect of distance education. It equalizes the playing field, giving time and space to those who suffer from their absence in a live setting, thereby becoming a place for unheard voices who now find an extended readership.

With the instructor orchestrating, affirming, building community and encouraging both participation and autonomy, this form of instruction has tremendous potential as a tool for teaching language and culture. The wide range of topics and activity that are feasible within this format also contribute to widening the range of discourses learners can sample and in which learners can participate.

SOME CONCEPTUAL GUIDELINES

As we've seen throughout this chapter, online correspondence has much to offer the language teacher and learner. The following are some broad guidelines you may wish to review and reflect on as part of your task design and implementation processes for telecommunications:

The tasks that prompt and sustain online communication need to be as interesting and relevant to learners as offline tasks in order to maintain a high level of interest and involvement.

- Tasks must merit the amount of time participants must invest in getting to a machine (perhaps even purchasing a machine and modem), reading, thinking, and composing on a regular basis.

- Participants in the online communication must be made to feel that what they have to contribute is valuable.

- Participants must be made to feel a level of ease and comfort with the forum so that their ideas and messages flow freely.

- Like in the classroom, online communication participants need to be made to feel they are learning the target language as a part of the online communication. Tasks with specific language/cultural foci and the ongoing mediation of the instructor are essential in this respect.

- The role of the instructor is critical in establishing and maintaining communications, drawing attention to uses, forms and functions of the target language, and serving as a court of appeals or arbiter for discussions. She is, in short, very, very active in this environment.

In a sense, online communication combines the best of all worlds for language learners in that they can simultaneously experience the comfort of conversational flow in the target language while still having the luxury of extra time to process and respond to what they read on the screen. They are also afforded a unique opportunity to be heard.

SUMMARY

The possibilities for active, constructive interactions using the target language abound with online communication. Modes of interaction range from simply communicating asynchronously with text only to live videoconferencing around shared onscreen workspaces. In either case, the nexus of the technology-supported activity is human communication and, as such, the kind of target language production and comprehension that can only serve to benefit students of additional languages. Reading, writing, and communicating asynchronously using text alone, like offline reading, writing, and speaking, can be rich in images and highly engaging. Synchronous telecommunications afford rich communicative experience whereby the learner can hone linguistic competency through authentic written and aural communicative activity. Telecommunications makes the sense of an interlocutor, a conversation partner, a reader, more immediate while allowing time to reflect on the messages one wants to convey to her and how hers are interpreted. These messages are typically composed with the craft and care of the traditional print letter, adhering to conventions appropriate to the message's reader and the writer's intent. These telecommunications "conventions" are partially appropriated from a writer's experiences as a reader, writer, and speaker of offline language, and are partially evolved and evolving ways of communicating in a medium which is somewhere in between the two.

Using telecommunications, language learners can practice a variety of languages, a wide range of registers and dialects, and gain a first-hand feel for the target culture and its peoples. They have access to many corners of the globe whereby to broaden their perspective and understanding of who they are as learners and speakers of additional languages.

Activities

For Discussion

Learners can practice a broad range of language skills in ways that complement the **CFA** heuristic. Brainstorm methods for learners to practice their reading, writing, listening, speaking, and pronunciation using online tools.

To Lurk or Not to Lurk...

Eavesdropping is a central, critical part of learning another language. Listening-in and trying to make sense of what one hears is not only legitimate, it is essential. Fortunately for language learners, in the world of telecommunications eavesdropping, or 'lurking,' is mostly acceptable. Learners can anonymously monitor information and exchanges of all kinds – something they were unable to do until the web came along. A discussion with students about the act of lurking (eavesdropping), its importance to their learning, some strategies for doing so well, and the ethics of the activity, could be a rich activity that precedes or accompanies online work.

Basic Telecommunications Literacy

In terms of online **communication**, learners must be able to:
- contact individuals to:
  - ask a question
  - express opinions
  - provide advice
  - exchange information
  - respond to questions

- contact groups of people
- participate in collaborative projects
- understand intended and implied meanings in such communications

For **constructing** online information, learner must know how to:
- create web pages and web sites using a variety of media
- manage web sites
- market web sites (let others know they're there)
- abide by copyright and intellectual property regulations

For **researching** online, learners need the following skills:
- developing a researchable question (determining keywords and categories)
- finding information using indices and search engines
- determining the level of quality and authority of information
- citing online resources appropriately

For each of the above three competencies – communication, constructing, and researching – devise activities that help the language learner demonstrate mastery of these competencies in the target language.

Composing Online

Prewriting/Brainstorming
When we compose, online or off, there is a certain kind of thinking that goes on prior to and while we bat out that first draft. This prewriting/brainstorming phase helps us decide what we think is important enough to write about and how it should be constructed. Here is a brainstorming activity learners can undertake either in the native or target language to get them centered on what they wish to say and how.

To use the cubing technique online, set up a text file something like the following:

1) Describe it
2) Compare it
3) Apply it
4) Contradict it
5) Contrast it
6) Defend it

The one firm rule for this activity is that students' fingers do not stop typing for any of the three minutes allotted for each side of the cube. They must write continuously about an object (I use a piece of candy of some kind; you can select any small object). The point is to let the imagination flow as the fingers move on the keyboard. At the end of each three minutes, have students review carefully what they have just written and determine what the *it* now is – the center of gravity for what it is they want to say – and use this as the *it* for the following side of the cube.

You can have students use this tool for prewriting brainstorming in any number of ways. For example, give them a diskette to take home or to a lab and have them pre-write/brainstorm on their own. Present the brainstorming heuristic as a stimulus in a networked lab setting where students can not only brainstorm their own thinking, but share with others at the same time.

Building Multimodal Texts

For the purposes of this text, multimedia design, like word processing, is considered a form of electronic communications. The rationale behind this categorization is that when engages in multimodal design, the intent is typically to communicate with others. For mediated language learning, it can be considered yet another tool through, about, and with which powerful forms of communication and language practice can take place.

What do L2 learners need to know about multimedia design? Not much they don't already know quite well. Anyone who watches TV, reads magazines and newspapers, and does retail consumption is intimately acquainted with multimodal message construction. Take the test yourself:

Study a product or advertisement and ask yourself about the following:

- the placement of primary, secondary, and tertiary information;
- the relative size, shape, and color of this information;
- other attention-getting techniques.

APPENDIX: FOR FURTHER READING AND INFORMATION

Betram, B., Peyton, J., and Bateson, T. (1993) (Eds) *Network-based classrooms: Promises and realities.* NY: Cambridge University Press.

Bolter, J. (1989) Beyond word processing: the computer as a new writing space. *Language and Communication*, 9, 2/3, 129-42.

Cummins, J. and Sayers, D. (1997) *Brave new schools: Challenging cultural illiteracy.* New York: St. Martin's Press.

Greenia, G. (1992) Computers and teaching composition in a foreign language. *Foreign Language Annals*, 25 (1) 33-46.

Sperling, D. (1998). (2nd Ed.). *Dave Sperlings's Internet guide.* Upper Saddle River, NJ: Prentice Hall. (800) 428-5331

Turkle, S. (1995) *Life on the screen: identify in the age of the Internet.* New York: Simon & Schuster.

Warschauer, M. and Kern, R. (2000) (Eds) *Network-based language teaching: Concepts and practice.* New York: Cambridge University Press.

Wood, A. and Smith, M. (2001) *Online communication: Linking technology, identity, and culture.* Mahwah, NJ: Lawrence Erlbaum.

For Resources Concerning Netiquette

http://www.albion.com/netiquette/corerules.html

For Online Learning Resources

For comprehensive information and links to online learning resources, try these very dense and interesting sites:

http://www.merlot.org
http://www.nflc.org

Asynchronous and Learning Management Tools

Moodle
http://www.moodle.com
A free open-course learning management system teachers can use to create their online courses.

Synchronous Tools
In addition to a number of messaging programs, WIMBA and Elluminate both allow classes to be help in synchronous time.

WIMBA
http://www.wimba.com

Elluminate
http://www.elluminate.com

8. Multimedia: Spaces, Performances, and Characters

There is nothing in the mind that wasn't first in the senses.
Aristotle

*Ultimately it's the pictures in our heads that matter,
not the ones on the screen.*
Reeves & Nass, 1997

Think of all the contexts in which you've read or heard the term *multimedia*: entertainment, education, business, telecommunications, art... It's difficult to imagine a realm of modern life in which the term has not been used for some purpose or another. The word tends to conjure a sense of frenetic sensory activity being stimulated by "high technology." Additionally, by virtue of 'heightened activity' and "high technology" there also accompanies the word multimedia a sense of awe, transcendence, super processing, and superior cognition. However, the term *multi* ("many") *media* ("more than one medium") might be applied to something as technologically simple as a slide projector show accompanied by recorded audio. Even captioned television and the reading aloud of illustrated stories (visual & auditory & textual) fall under this basic definition. But contemporary conjuring of the term *multimedia* most likely results in a computer display with text, images, animations, audio, and video combined for some informational, entertainment, or amusement purpose. There is some optimism that these ways of combining media have the potential to refresh our communication forms by making new juxtapositions of images, texts, and sounds possible.

Beyond the obvious benefit that combined forms of representation hold for supporting second language learning, what is particularly pertinent is that computers allow some compelling control over the media they can display. As we have discussed in earlier chapters, it is this control/manipulation that is in many ways at the heart of multimedia uses in language teaching and learning. This notion of 'control' extends from the physical manipulation to the critical assessments of what one sees, hears, and reads in a multimedia environment.

A central aspect of things 'multisensory' is that we humans appear to be particularly well wired to process audiovisual information. Our inheritance from several hundred thousands of years of "being on the lookout" (for food and danger) have paid off in a brain anatomy that is not only wired to see and hear acutely, but a very sophisticated system of referring to these processes linguistically. Take, for example, the fact that there is a disproportionate amount of vocabulary in all human languages that relate to the audiovisual. An astounding two-thirds to three-fourths of all words describing the work of our senses are related to hearing and vision. It is not happenstance, therefore, that we have recently evolved ever more sophisticated ways of fashioning, combining, and making more complex fodder for our eyes and ears.

Regarding the impact of human contact with contemporary multiple media (lots of visual and aural happening at once on a screen), there are two different schools of thought. When it comes to the effects of 'multimodal' processing, there are those who see *more* as *better* and those who see *more* as *too much*. For the former, the thinking goes that understanding is enhanced by material in multiple formats—more cognitive engagement being required to evoke understanding in multiple modalities. The auditory reinforces the visual which reinforces the textual with the accompanying mental processes engaged in continual comprehension and cross-check. The latter school of thought — *more is too much* — views material requiring auditory, visual, and textual processing as too demanding and — as you may have experienced with many commercial websites — too confusing and distracting. Even though at any given time we tend to focus on one modality over others, in these environments there is the inherent risk of distraction and distortion. In either case, it is the premise of this chapter that language professionals can exploit these multiple media for their own purposes – target language acquisition for their students.

OPPORTUNITIES FOR L2 COMMUNICATION

Combined media represent opportunity for motivated comprehension, collaboration, and engagement in meaningful, productive discourse. We typically view work within multimedia (instructional or entertainment software packages or Internet sites) as solitary, autonomous activity. But there are many social dimensions to multimedia that need to be carefully considered in designing and using the medium, and that can be nicely exploited for language learning activities.

Mixing and allowing learners to manipulate combined media carries a host of implications. Assistance in understanding some of these implications comes from the field of media studies that, in its brief history, has turned up some informative findings about our relationship with new media. Brief descriptions of the social dimensions of this relationship follow. These are based on a comprehensive review and synthesis of current research in human-media interaction undertaken by Reeves & Nass (1996). The umbrella concept of the Reeves and Nass research is that, to we humans, *mediated life is the same as real life*. That is, how we react to what we see, hear, and read on the screen resembles how we react to reality in general, and to others in society in particular. These social dimensions will be taken up in discussion and examples of language learning activity involving multimedia material. They can be summarized as follows:

- we respond to motion
- we respond to close proximity (e.g., close-ups)
- politeness counts (we see the machine as a social participant that needs to exhibit socially appropriate behavior)
- we respond to arousal (a little helps memory, too much and we shut down)
- casting counts (we attend to those most like us and those cast as 'experts')
- we respond positively to praise and flattery (negatively to criticism)
- the social skills of characters depicted are more valued than IQ
- negative characteristics and events are more salient to memory than positive

All of these features of human-media interaction are useful to understand on many fronts: when designing materials, when responding to materials, and as a source of discussion on the topic of media and representation, for example. Where some or all of these features may be intuitive, they make for good guidelines and foci for language learning activities. What follows is a discussion of each of these media features along with implications for teaching and learning.

We respond to motion: We respond to close proximity
Both the motion and proximity of objects and people carry social meaning in real life. As teachers, for example, we use these devices intuitively in the social act of orchestrating our instruction. According to Reeves and Nass, there is a great deal of empirical evidence that indicates that this type of reaction to motion and proximity carries over to what happens on the computer screen. Learners using multimedia computer software or Internet sites will react similarly: they will be aroused by and attend more carefully to what *moves* and to what is *close* and large on the screen.

These features can be exploited much as we exploit the characteristics of other realia we choose to use. One way to begin thinking about ways to capitalize on the strength of the motion/proximity response is to consider it in relation to **F**orm, **C**ommunication, and **A**ffect. Because motion and proximity heighten our attention and awareness, they can be capitalized on in directing and reinforcing learner attention to the specific forms, representations, and discourse related to these. Such activity, as discussed in Chapter 1, is a desirable part of the language learning enterprise. Attention and awareness are directed at important **F**orms in the target language during communicative activities. Likewise for the element of **C**ommunication, the features of motion and proximity can be conceived as powerful focal points and anchors for motivated talk. Further, because the motion/proximity response is a largely subconscious and affective one, guidance in critical consumption – being aware of how forms are used to manipulate – is equally important.

Politeness counts
Studies of human-computer interaction show that we respond to the ways in which machines are designed to communicate with us in much the same way as we respond to human interlocutors. That is, we see computers as social partners and, as such, if rules of polite behavior are violated, we react negatively. If machines use politeness techniques in their communications, we respond positively. We've all heard ourselves or others talking (not always politely) to computers. Part of the social pact or set of expectations of human-computer interaction is that the machine responds to our actions in ways we feel are appropriate and can anticipate. This is clearly not always the case, and we react accordingly. This phenomenon represents opportunity in second language teaching in that learners' attention and awareness can be guided to the principles of polite, rude, and unanticipated interaction. These communication principles (Grice's Maxims) are summarized in Chapter 7. In the context of multimedia, learners use these maxims as an ongoing guide when analyzing software, sites, and their own discourse with and around these. By focusing in on the communicative aspects of the machine's 'social behavior,' attention can be drawn to the **F**orms of appropriate (polite) interaction, a critical aspect in the development of communicative competence.

We respond to arousal
Things large and moving on a screen arouse us. Additional features of screen representation also lead to arousal (e.g., color, sound, etc.). Empirical findings from the fields of psychology and media studies indicate that where *a little* bit of arousal indeed helps to stimulate and make salient key information for long-term memory, *too much* arousal

causes us to shut down, to become passive, to not attend. Many commercial software packages and websites fall into this category of overkill when it comes to arousal. Too much sound, color, movement, and odd or surprising content in combination causes more of a hypnotic than an attentive state. As educators, we can select to avoid multimedia material like this or instruct and guide learners to recognize this effect and use it as a point of discovery and discussion.

Casting counts
That we respond to those most like us and to those depicted as "experts" is no news to any critical consumer of media. Likewise, the credibility we ascribe a multimedia character correlates with:

1) the degree to which they most resemble us as individuals and those in our immediate community (thus, the Walter Chronkite effect for the white, middle class majority in the U.S.); and,

2) the appearance that they are somehow 'credentialed' and have authority.

Probing the issue of identification and credibility with learners can tune their attention to the visual appearance and delivery of a multimedia character and their individual responses to it. Within these appearances and deliveries attention can be drawn to the ways in which larger-than-life manufactured characters use language to meet their communicative agendas, be it 'sincerity,' 'expertise,' or 'compassion.' How characteristics of 'expertise' are similarly and differently constituted across cultures is also valuable to explore with learners.

We respond positively to praise and flattery (negatively to criticism)
Early on in the history of technology in education, when personal computers started to become commonplace in learning institutions, one feature more than any other captured the attention of educators and pundits: *feedback*. That the computer could play the role of an interactive tutor—telling a learner when she got a right or wrong answer, and even explaining why—was an aspect that was initially seen as holding great promise in education and training. This enthusiasm didn't, and typically still doesn't, consider the broader social nature of the human-computer conversation; one that, through media studies, we understand to consist of the human interlocutor reacting and responding to the machine as if the silicon were actually playing a social role. If the computer praises or flatters, we respond positively, as we would in interaction with other

humans. If the computer criticizes or indicates any negativity towards us (including thwarting our efforts to accomplish something!), our reaction is strong and negative.

The implications for teaching and learning with multimedia are many in this regard. Critical media literacy skills, including learner understanding that these simulated 'conversations' with the machine are just that—simulated— are a good place to start. The personalities of multimedia characters can be troubleshot and analyzed along with learners' reactions to them. This is a rich source of discourse around the more complex interpersonal side of communicating in the target language that is enhanced by the multimedia features of *start, stop, zoom in, link,* etc. In short, the dialectical relationship between learner and multimedia depictions can be exploited for expanding critical awareness of both media attributes and language in action. Our natural responses to the positive and negative can serve as a powerful jumping off point for such activity.

The social skills of characters depicted are more valued than IQ
More and more, our understandings of what we see and hear on screens is tending to the superficial. We react more to the way people appear in terms of hair, dress, demeanor, and personality than we do to deeper intellectual qualities or messages. Studying what constitutes valued superficial and intellectual qualities in target language/culture characters is, again, a powerful exercise supported by multimedia tools and features. How those depicted in multimedia software and websites are reacted to within the target culture and from outside (the L2 community) makes for fascinating discussion, analyses, and expanded understandings of language in action.

Negative characters, events are more salient to memory than positive
At first blush you may consider this one of the sorrier aspects of the human condition. It is, however, very real and one that media-using educators should be attuned to and ready to harvest for teaching and learning. Termed the "law of hedonic asymmetry," it is our propensity to respond strongly to, and to remember the negative more than the positive. It is a fact of life much exploited by politicians, The Media, and the entertainment industry. For the multimedia-using educator, it is an important universal to be considered in lesson planning, testing, and moment-by-moment teaching and learning activity. It also represents a wealth of possibilities for discussion and values clarification work.

Multimedia software and website developers are not ignorant of this fact of human nature. This is why in children's software, where attention spans run short and attention is critical for the perceived success of a product, you will see a lot of spilling, dropping, tripping, crashing, flashing, and the like. Likewise, in materials designed for adolescents and adults, there is frequently evil, violence, and perversion. Turning learner attention to both the presence of the negative in mediated learning and to their reaction to it is fuel for lively discussion, reflection, and self-realization. In reviewing multimedia materials to incorporate into the language curricula there is certainly the temptation to go for what is the liveliest, the snazziest. After all, there is some basic logic in engaging as many facets of mind as possible. Go ahead and use the snazziest, but take it on as any other tool: that is, thoughtfully with your larger goals and concerns in mind. Design tasks accordingly.

A closer look at the detail of the special features afforded by multimedia takes us to examine its micro-forms and functions rather than those broader features described in the above section. When we zoom in on what we see and manipulate on contemporary computer screens, be it multimedia and/or telecommunications, there are characteristics of that visual and aural material that hold special value for language teaching and learning. Because the bulk of this multimedia material now resides and will reside in ever greater quantity on the Internet, the following section examines the nature and exploitability of this phenomenal resource.

MULTIMEDIATED COMMUNICATION

Few would argue that the best thing about the Internet is 'connections'—connecting up with people directly through e-mail, chat sites, social networking sites, blogs, and gaming and indirectly through common interests in readily sharable information. Indeed, the results of survey after survey, as well as online tracking, conclude that the vast majority of what gets done on the Internet is human-to-human communication. Add the communications capability of the Internet, the opportunity to include links to any media object (pictures, film clips, music, animations, interactive games), and even the objects themselves, and you have rich possibilities for language learners to discuss these lively objects with others. Co-viewing, co-building, and co-manipulating multimedia materials can work to enrich the constructionist aspect of language acquisition. Such activities open up the perceptual channels (aural, visual) to be included in what is otherwise a text-based conversation. Reference to and manipulation of these perceptual elements can serve as anchors to target language exchanges. As such, "shared" multimedia experiences on the Internet are natural venues for second language communication practice.

Just like the world at large, the professional educator must sort through materials and make use of what is at hand. Language professionals have a history of doing this. We examine the world and exploit it for teaching the language that accompanies and defines it. We see knowledge not as something one can posses, but as a vehicle through which learners can come to own the language they use to make sense of what they experience. The flood of information on the web is a world that can be similarly exploited. It can be used as realia through and around which language skills can be practiced and honed. In terms of culture, moreover, learners of other languages can access so much information and entertainment that culture via the Internet is rivaled only by in-country-immersion-plus-expert-guide experiences!

THE CONE OF INSTRUCTION

By virtue of its multimodal and manipulable characteristics, the Internet makes possible a very wide range of learning activity. As represented in the adaptation of Dale's Cone of Experience (below), the Internet potentially encompasses not only all of the types of learning listed, but in myriad combinations.

Note that these abstract, iconic, and enactive learning types were, prior to widespread use of the Internet, treated as separate, distinct, and as affecting very different modes of learning. From direct, purposeful experiences (chatting with others, accessing needed information) to creating, manipulating, and comprehending abstract verbal symbols of all kinds, the Internet combines these into multimediated forms. The possibilities for developing instructional activities that involve multiple modalities and a range of experience types are infinite.

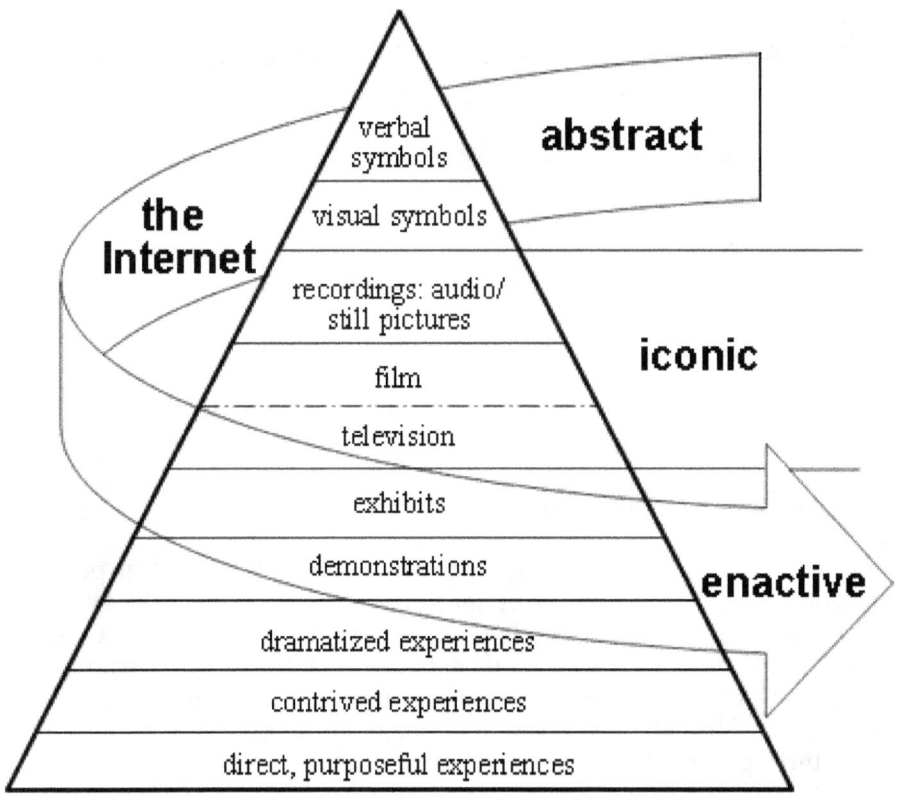

Adapted from "The Cone" (Dale, 1969)

ANALOGOUS SPACES[6]

Where can you begin to consider this range and wealth of linguistic and cultural opportunity for your language learners? The following *analogous spaces* can be used as a conceptual starting point. As a whole these spaces make up a broad framework for considering the potential exploitation of commonplace Internet resources for language instruction purposes. They are listed here, then examined in more detail. They are:

- **interrogation space:** A place where information can be interrogated (searched)

---

[6] A version of Analogous Spaces originally appeared in Meskill, C. (1999)

- **workbook:** a place where questions and exercises are undertaken

- **storybook :** a place where stories can be read, heard, and explored

- **creation space:** a place for writing, creating visual representations, publishing and archiving

- **virtual world:** a simulated environment

- **dialogic space:** a place to communicate with others

The Web as an Interrogation Space

Consideration of the Web as a vast repository of information points to the learning activity of extracting information as a logical strategy. Given what learners already know about the world, the linguistic and cultural benefits of their perusing and extracting specific information and bringing that information back to a group or the class as a whole to be reworked, reshaped, negotiated, presented, or discredited, for example, make these powerful language learning activities.

The Web as Workbook

Again, because there is so much and so much variety of material available on the web, the possibilities for creating, and having students create for one another, challenges with web materials are immense. Challenges can consist of appropriating text, images, and audio/video sequences and putting them in the service of any number of language learning activities. You and your students can cut/paste or download selected materials and design online tasks (cloze, comprehension routines, manipulation tasks, etc.) with them.

The Web as Storybook

Stories exist on the web in many forms, at many levels. The architecture of information itself can be considered a storyline of sorts: going from one piece of information to its link and back. Recounting web navigation stories, a task that requires the same level of craft and linguistic sophistication as oral or written stories of a more traditional type, can be a powerful, motivated form of language practice. Additionally, a great deal of material on the web *is* story—anything from people's personal histories to great works of literature. As such, these can be used as catalysts for eliciting students' responses just as offline works of literature are frequently used as part of the language learning process.

The Web as Creation Space

Creating and composing using web resources is engaging activity in that it involves learners in a range of productive uses of the target language. In a classroom/laboratory context, moreover, the process of that creation is public and therefore represents a springboard for talk around and about the creation process itself. Web materials that have been cut/pasted or downloaded can be modified and combined in any number of ways as a language learning task. Collaborative creativity can be orchestrated in physical contexts where learners can work together and they can take place via telecommunications where learners can co-build shared sites and the like.

The Web as Virtual World

More and more, the web is providing virtual experiences. Learners can immerse themselves in the forests and shopping malls in the countries whose language and culture they study. "Inside" these worlds, learners can explore, gather, and query novel environments. Tasks that motivate learners to engage in this kind of thinking—thinking that is based in the language and culture represented within these virtual worlds—comprise excellent practice in motivated target language use.

Web as Dialogic Space

A great deal of attention has been given the human-to-human communications aspects of the web. Its role as a dialogic space, where people who would not otherwise be able or likely to communicate can now link up, has been cited as its most powerful attribute. Communications using the target language can take place locally (between members of a class, students in a building, or in any established newsgroup), or globally, through multiple chat facilities accessible on the web. Tasks designed to make use of this compelling facility can have learners engaging in extended dialogue using the target language and investigating the target culture in ways that make sense to larger course goals and processes.

Analogous spaces, such as those above, can serve as a conceptual tool when considering the ways the Internet can be exploited for language and culture learning. It is a method of viewing the vast and powerful resources on the web for the development of learner skills and understanding.

MULTIMEDIATED LISTENING

The plethora of aural materials available via the Internet, and the fact that these digital recordings can co-occur with visual information and be manipulated in any number of ways, make the medium a natural asset for listening skills development. In a multimedia environment, the possibilities for inviting students to do things before, during, and after listening in the target language are many and varied. Learner interaction with listening material might be limited to a learner indicating comprehension by selecting from multiple choice answers, or be as complex as learners using information and tools to construct thoughtful representations of their individual understandings of an aural text. In any case, learners are actively doing something, performing some action, in conjunction with, or in response to what they hear. This is called *Listening Performance*.

Brown (1994) defines Listening Performance as what language learners actually *do* during a listening activity. He defines six types of listening performance: reactive, intensive, responsive, selective, extensive, and interactive. These performance types progress from simple (reactive) to the most complex form of listening (interactive). There is a parallel continuum when types of user performance with computer-based multimedia are examined. These range from simple reacting to on-screen or aural input (reactive) to complex interaction with material through manipulation and construction (interactive).

Reactive listening performance

Reactive listening performance focuses on surface aspects of the language, not necessarily understanding. A prevalent example of this kind of listening is choral response listening where students directly mimic or perform simple transformations on what a teacher says. A multimedia example of reactive listening is when a student is prompted to repeat or make transformations on what gets 'spoken' by the system. This can be achieved by having students 'speak' to the screen, type in what they hear, or click the mouse on a pictorial or textual representation of what is heard.

Intensive listening performance

Intensive performance requires learners to concentrate on the component parts of what they hear. This may take the form of listening to a teacher repeat a sentence and indicating the form of the verb or intonation pattern she is using. A multimedia example of intensive listening would be colorizing. In a multimedia presentation where text accompanies audio and/or video, the user can be prompted to focus on component parts of sentences when these parts are visually marked by color. The user can also be prompted to listen for specific components and type them in or colorize them to indicate successful discrimination.

Responsive listening performance

Responsive performance requires students to listen to a teacher's question or cue and respond immediately and appropriately, thereby indicating understanding. Teacher prompts can take the form of *meaningful questions* (Where were you yesterday?), *commands* (Please close that door.), *clarifications* (What did she say?), and *comprehension checks* (Do you mean she was sick?). In terms of *meaningful questions*, multimedia systems are limited. Computers are currently limited in their processing of and response to natural input. However, the system can certainly pose such questions, prompt the student to type in or record a response, and save these as files for a peer or teacher to assess. Only the most advanced of voice recognition software allows for limited aural conversation between the speaker and computer, provided the dialogue stays within the confines of programmed script. On the other hand, responding to *commands* is a performance perfectly suited for multimedia systems. The learner can respond to audio commands in any number of ways: clicking on the screen, moving objects around on the screen, starting and stopping an audio or video segment as commanded, typing in predetermined words or sentences, and the like.

Responding to requests for *clarification* is also feasible in a multimedia environment. Requests for clarification (Are you sure?, Do you mean X?, etc.) can be simulated auditorily, textually, and/or by a video character. The learner has only to provide clarification in ways similar to those suggested for responding to commands. Demonstrating *comprehension* is also readily feasible with this form of instructional technology. Comprehension can be indicated in response to multimedia prompts through typing or clicking with corresponding feedback provided.

Selective listening performance

Selective performance requires learners to listen to longer stretches of discourse for the purpose of getting specific information from the aural text. Multimedia also accommodates this listening performance well and easily. Learners can be prompted to listen selectively for particular information, then to indicate successful identification of this information by typing in or selecting appropriate key words, pictures, or sequences from a group of possible selections. The learner can also manipulate elements on the screen in response to successful selective listening.

Extensive listening performance

Extensive listening requires fuller understanding of lengthier aural texts for the purpose of in-depth understanding. This form of listening is especially well suited for multimedia in that the learner, unlike in real-time situations, can control the rate and sequence of the aural presentation. She can also make use of visual and textual clues available in a multimedia format to understand what she hears. On-line note taking capabilities, access to supporting information, and the availability of tools (key word guidance, a dictionary, and the like) add to the suitability of the medium for extensive listening. Learner performance can take the forms described in previous sections, only requiring more extensive, in-depth understanding.

Interactive listening performance

Interactive performance calls into play the above types of listening performance in face-to-face interaction. As the full negotiation of meaning that takes place between human interlocutors is not realizable between a learner and a multimedia system, the option of using the technology as a springboard for student-student interaction becomes an option. Individual work with listening skills development can, moreover, be viewed as needed rehearsal for human interaction in the target language.

By interacting with multimedia software and Internet resources, students can practice a wide range of listening skills. This easily accessible material also makes it possible and practical to integrate a listening-focus with other learning activity.

SUMMARY

The combined visual, auditory, and textual materials in conjunction with the manipulability of these materials constitute multimedia. Such resources offer extensive opportunity for target language acquisition and target culture contact. With the visual and textual referencing and supporting learner comprehension and performances, the learning activity is enriched, and the learner empowered. Such formats stimulate our natural tendencies to make optimal use of the visual and aural in combination to assess the world and solve immediate problems. As such, multimedia can be viewed as complementary not only to the **Form** end of the language learning heuristic, but the **Affect** dimension as well.

Activities

Look About...

Create a multimedia Rorschach. This can be done by cutting and pasting text and images into a *PowerPoint* or *Adobe* record and analyze the language that ensues when you ask others what they see.

Think About...

Contemporary media is engaging 'old brains.' That is, the time for our reactions to develop is only as long as these media have been in existence, as opposed to the thousands of years we've had to develop responses to our social and physical environment. What are some cognitive consequences of this 'old brain' / 'new forms' encounter? What are the inherent implications for learning additional languages?

Talk About...

What does our relationship with screens imply in terms of language? Does it in some way mimic our negotiations with texts? with other humans?

Building Multimedia Resources

It's understood in the language profession that when we speak of culture we speak of two distinct genres of "cultural understandings." One is Big C culture, the other is Little c culture.

> *Culture*: music, art, architecture, Customs (holidays, food, costumes)
>
> *culture*: the beliefs and norms that determine practices in everyday life (e.g., learning, relationships, getting things done, time, money, etc.)

Video footage is readily accessible and manipulable on and through the Internet. Students and teachers work together to assemble and annotate representations of the everyday workings of the cultures of the world depicted in video. Images representing aspects such as

- Home life
- Values/perceptions
- Ethics
- Etiquette

are manifest in everyday language and behaviors. These are Little *c* cultural material. Material concerning the great art and customs of the wealthy are considered Big *C* material. Both can benefit from cross social and cultural analysis and annotation.

Video representations can be a tremendous tool to stimulate thinking about and probing further the different ways people live in the world based on their values and beliefs. Critical analysis of the microlevel norms and behaviors portrayed in television and film are valuable in developing understandings about the target culture and one's own. Collect digital clips from film and TV, or use full texts. Then students and teachers can edit these to represent and support their observations about cultural similarities and differences. You and your students can maintain an expanding, annotated database of video observations about the target language and culture. Such a database can be used in class and by others too in their research for presentations, essays, and productions.

Universals/Representations
In 1945, George Murdock listed the following 67 universals of culture:

age-grading
athletic sports
bodily adornment
calendar
cleanliness training
community organization

cooking
cooperative labor
cosmology
courtship
dancing
decorative art
divination
division of labor
dream interpretation
education
eschatology (beliefs
    concerning death)
ethics
ethno-botany
etiquette
faith
healing
family feasting
fire-making
folklore
food taboos
funeral rites
games
gestures
fight giving
government
greetings
hair styles
hospitality

hygiene
incest taboos
inheritance rules
joking
kin groups
kinship nomenclature
language
law
luck superstitions
magic
marriage
mealtimes
medicine
obstetrics
penal sanctions
personal names
population policy
postnatal care
pregnancy usages
property rights
propitiation of
    supernatural beings
puberty customs
religious ritual
residence rules
sexual restrictions
soul concepts
status differentiation
surgery
tool making
trade
visiting
weather control
weaving

Part 1: Choose three of these. Find a website that pertains to each of the three; each must be from a non-US culture. Links to the sites should be part of your response. Your response will consist of a comparison and contrast of the three elements you've selected in the three cultures you have selected. How are they the same/different from your own? from one another? What are the implications of these similarities and differences in cross-cultural understanding and global affairs? What about these similarities and differences might be important for you to include in your own teaching?

Part 2: As you are undertaking Part 1, keep a running log of your strategies. What steps did you lay out in advance? How did you proceed from step to step? What were some of the contingencies for how you progressed? Finally, which steps, processes, and thoughts that you undertook, do you think are valuable to teach as part of new literacy?

APPENDIX: RESOURCES FOR LISTENING MATERIALS ON THE WEB

Randall's ESL Cyber Listening Lab
http://esl-lab.com
A wide array of graded listening sequences with accompanying multiple choice quizzes that can be submitted for immediate scoring.

Merlot World Language Discipline Community
http://merlot.org
Hundreds of links to foreign language listening resource materials.

9. Electronic Literacy as a Second Language

The illiterate of the 21st century will not be those who cannot read and write, but those who cannot learn, unlearn, and relearn.
Alvin Toffler

We are drowning in information, while starving for wisdom.
Edward O. Wilson

Definitions

literacies: modes of communication (dynamic, shifting representations) that take on meaning within given social/political/cultural contexts

electronic texts—information of all kinds—aural, visual—that appears electronically on a computer screen

---

LITERACIES

Throughout these chapters, we have probed various ways that learners of additional languages are afforded opportunities to engage in Communication with, through, and around media and technologies. The main purpose for this engagement is, of course, to gain the requisite skills and competencies they need to operate effectively in the language and culture they are learning. "Operating effectively" is what is in part considered "literacy." In this chapter, issues related to second language literacy – the ability to communicate in an additional language – and literacy in the narrower sense of being able to read and write in contemporary electronic environments – what we will call *electronic literacy* – will be progressively interwoven. The end goal is an integrated frame of second language literacy that includes the specialized forms of literacy that are hypothetically inherent in new, multimedia technologies, and that involve language learners in new forms of reading, writing, speaking, and listening. In short, at the beginning of the twenty-first century, electronic literacy ought to be considered part and parcel of the second language learning enterprise both as a language acquisition tool and as a learning outcome.

Let's start with the term *literacy*. It is commonplace to see the word *computer* attached to the word *literacy* for "computer literacy." This collocation is an attempt to capture what we commonly think of as "screen literacy"—what contemporary computer users need to know to operate a machine (e.g., pointing and clicking in an intentioned manner, knowing how and what to type in a dialogue box, and the like). You can be fairly confident that contemporary students possess this "screen literacy" and that if they don't, that they can very quickly master it. Moreover, lessons in basic screen literacy make for marvelous language learning activities, such as task-based listening practice in identification and movement in a Windows/Internet environment.

Electronic literacy is distinct from and extends well beyond this basic screen literacy. Like print literacy, electronic literacy entails being able to develop and exercise understandings in consort with authored material. Like 'ink-reading,' *e-texting* is the act of making meaning with signs and symbols assembled for the purpose of communicating. In the case of electronic literacy, what one "reads" extends beyond the written word to include graphics, audio, and video and invites a number of physical actions on the part of the 'reader' that make "e-texting" unique from traditional print reading.

Both print and electronic reading require interaction; both forms require *work* on the part of the reader. In either format, simply locating a clip, message, passage, or other 'piece' does not constitute the act of reading, an act that entails contemplation and reaching understanding within and beyond what one reads. Many have argued that there is more risk of superficial encounters in an electronic text environment given the constraints by, and manner in which, one interacts. Indeed, the limited space of a single screen typically forces electronic text into tight packets (boxes, icons, screens within screens) – in short, condensed visual information. This is not to say that print, or ink reading, cannot be similarly presented: cereal boxes and newspaper advertisements, for example, are also subject to restrictions in size. The work that a reader does in either case can consist of simply glossing or accessing packets of information, or it can be sustained, thoughtful interaction with the intended and interpreted meanings of the text. This implies that the usual attack skills that one applies to print reading need to be modified and expanded to accommodate these packets in their various forms and with their various purposes. The higher level thinking required to filter, select, and integrate these into synthetic, useful conceptual pieces is certainly an important skill to consider in language learning and teaching both from the point of view of training these skills and of making use of them in learning activity.

E-literacy as Choice

Choice is an integral part of language learning processes. It exercises the identity of the individual acting in the target language. It renders learning active. It exercises the democratic. It respects diversity of views and interests. It is something that can be defended. And it makes one think. Since electronic texts first appeared on the screens of computers, the choice-factor in human-computer interaction, especially when it was seen as "student control over learning," has been an often lauded feature of the medium when it is used for instruction. Not only do learners have a choice in what they will do overall, but they also exercise the same kind of choice/decision making that will provide them feedback from the machine (recall the machine-user interface discussion in Chapter 6). Expanding this notion of e-texts beyond this machine-user interaction, we can include the broader notions of choice as part of the language learning enterprise.

At the most basic level of text/e-text interaction, readers/e-texters make choices as to whether they attend to the Form of the text (the words, appearance, style, and the like), or the meaning the text conveys. This is true of both ink and electronic symbols. It is also what makes texts such an enduring tool for the language instructional process. The direct connections made between abstract symbols (e.g., words) and that to which they refer are a cornerstone of language instruction. Choice in what we attend to, the degree of attention we pay along the Form-meaning continuum, is determined and steered by the teaching professional and the task she designs and orchestrates with her learners. With the explosion of available e-texts on the Internet, the issue of choice also becomes more complex and more critical for teachers. Fortunately for instructors, there are numerous clearinghouses and metapages that carry links to Internet resources and peer-reviewed lesson plans of sites deemed useful by colleagues in the field.

For learners, the development and honing of good, critical selection skills to apply in the face of so many available e-texts can be incorporated and encouraged as part of the instructional process. Learning to 'do e-text' as – or in – a second language is a thoroughly motivating and relevant activity for the language classroom. Moreover, learning to evaluate the source/authorship of an e-text can be an integral part of understanding the norms, values, and worldviews of the target culture. Judging who to believe and explicating why vary between languages and cultures. What does not vary, however, is our need to continually make judgements about the veracity of what we encounter on the web and the agenda of its authors. The more facile we become doing so in our own and across languages and cultures, the more e-literate we become.

FORM

Recall that in the tripartite heuristic for second language learning used throughout this text, Form is one of three critical, interacting components. The implications of the various forms of material used in mediated language learning – audio, video, multimedia – have been discussed in previous chapters. There are forms or features particular to electronic texts that are unique to them; that differ from print, as well as from stand-alone audiovisual materials.

These implications, along with the fundamental physical differences in Form between electronic texts (e-texts) and print, are summarized below:

Print	**E-texts**
unimodal	multimodal
static	dynamic, malleable
hierarchical	anarchic
self-contained	hyper, decentralized
linear	non-linear
whole	fragmentary
restrictive	democratizing
private activity	public activity

Print is unimodal in that it entails the processing of ink on paper whereas e-texts potentially involve the processing of images – both still and moving – and sound in conjunction with what is conventionally considered print/text. The implications this increase in modalities implies for language acquisition was discussed at some length in Chapter 8. Suffice it to say here that additional modes of processing greatly distinguish the act of reading from the act of e-texting. Likewise, the fact that e-texts are dynamic and malleable, as opposed to static print, can be viewed as contributing to a certain increased participation in e-texting in general, and language learning activity in particular. E-texters make active decisions regarding the shape, direction, and speed of what they are 'reading' that are not part of the ink reading process. In the e-text below, for example, all that is immediately visible can be reshaped by the e-texter at will (resized, rewindowed, rearranged). While the implications for language acquisition activities are many and powerful, perhaps the most salient is that learners are actively engaging with target language material rather than passively encountering it.

Not unrelated to the static/dynamic distinction is the fact that e-texts can be 'read' in any order, in any fashion, and be physically changed by the reader. This culminates in a type of anarchy, an attribute of second language learning activity that places control and responsibility in the hands of learners, not instructors. This anarchy is complimented by the decentralized (hypertextual) and non-linear organization of e-texts. Again, e-texters exert their choice, their will, their decisions on the relational aspect of what they 'read.' Rather than whole, linear tracts, the e-texter interacts with fragments that she assembles and makes sense of according to her immediate needs and goals. In this sense, e-texts can be viewed as being democratizing in contrast to the more restrictive print forms that lead one's reader down singular, linear, predetermined paths.

One aspect of the last print/e-text contrast on the above list—their potentially quite public nature – was taken up in the context of telecommunications in Chapter 7. In addition to the public voice one gains in telecommunications environments, there is also the aspect of publicness in public physical contexts where computers are used by language learners: classrooms, labs, libraries, pods, or public spaces. What one does on the screen in such environments is truly public, especially if instructors exploit and encourage that publicness. In this respect, e-texts become something that can be readily referred to, speculated about, and manipulated. With certain tasks and activities that integrate active peer/teacher involvement, what appears on a computer screen can inform and support language learning activities of all kinds.

Recreated here in print form (below), this e-text may not appear to possess all the attributes listed above it. When on a computer screen, however, it is indeed multimodal in that one can hear music, voices, and a selection of bleeps and bloops as part of its make up. As such it is dynamic in a direct, physical sense unlike static print. Central to this dynamism is the effect of a click on several of its visual components. The effect can be a direct sensory experience or a link to a different representation.

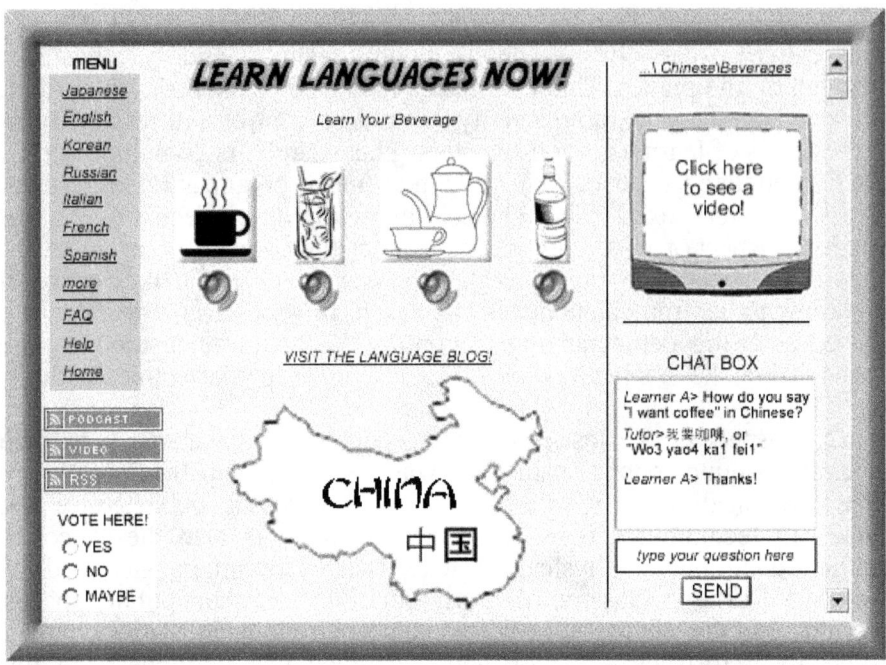

E-TEXTING

These differences in the form of electronic texts versus print carry implications for differences between reading print and "e-texting." Some have decried this shift from linear and hierarchical to anarchic as a dumbing down, a shortening of attention span and, consequently, a shift from depth to breadth in knowing and understanding. But, as hypertext author Michael Joyce argues, because e-texts are made up of constellations of information sourced from many voices, they require a different form of attention that he calls "successive attending" (Joyce, 1999). This contrasts sharply with the sustained linear attention required of print. As anthropologist Margaret Mead is noted for having observed, it is young children who demonstrate the directions human development in cognition and behavior are heading in the future. There is no question that children's facility with the successive attendings required by e-texts (and television!) is evidence of the direction our literacies are taking.

For second language learners, successive attending may offer some benefit in terms of the amount of information that needs to be stored from moment to moment when processing target language input.

The fact that e-texts are most typically represented in small bundles rather than sustained, linear pieces, and that the relationship between these bundles is spatial, may alleviate some pressure on short term memory for processing in the target language. The 'bundle effect' of e-texts can also be instructionally exploited in that the 'spaces' between bundles can be a source of productive talk and writing. In this way language learners can be guided to simultaneously focus on the Form e-texts take and the meanings they convey.

Also called "hyper-reading" (Sosnoski, 1999) e-texting is the act of making sense of MTV-like rapid-fire juxtaposed images and making sense of what one 'reads' on hyper-informative Internet pages. Unlike linear print where readers select their own interstices for digesting, reflecting, imagining, and rewriting, these hyper-environments force quick connections that are, in comparison to those crafted by print authors for readers to see and identify with, quite arbitrary and idiosyncratic.

Reading	**E-texting**
previewing	limited (can't see whole picture)
scanning	"
determine what to read first	"
determine what to read in detail	determine what to print out/save to file
determine what to ignore	more to be ignored (potentially extraneous to immediate and long-term purposes)
glosses, annotations, dog ears	cut, paste, size, mark-up, link, juxtapose, delete

Some differences between reading and e-texting

It has been widely contended that an increase in the mobility and malleability of text would logically influence thought and, by extension, our expression of thought in language. The amount and type of thinking involved with multimodal forms involves more and differing kinds of mental processes: visual reasoning, text reasoning, manipulation reasoning, aural reasoning. It can and has been argued that the addition of these 'other modality' features may constitute less mental work than print reading. When reading print, the aural and visual is left to the reader's imagination and interpretation – activity that is traditionally considered "high load"—as opposed to looking at a picture referred to directly by an aural text. The jury is still out on this issue in general, but in terms of second language learning these extra modalities are widely viewed as supportive of comprehension and, by extension, acquisition of the target language. If the aural or textual code is inadequate for understanding, the thinking goes, the addition of a visual version can support understanding those codes. Likewise, the thinking and talk that can be orchestrated around multimodal representations can be supported and enhanced by virtue of their multifacetedness.

It's fairly safe to say that reading e-texts is unlike reading print in the traditional sense. No one that I know reads screens from top to bottom, left to right. On the contrary, we scan for the general layout, the gist of the page we are viewing, consider our options based on our goals and prior knowledge, and proceed accordingly. If there is some extended information (e.g., a map, a list, or a lengthy text), we may choose to print it out and use our traditional print/visual literacy to make sense of these as traditional print. Like a print reader, in order to be a successful e-texter, one must possess the following:

- a fairly extensive knowledge of vocabulary and syntax;
- an understanding of the organizational options and meanings they carry;
- competencies in monitoring, predicting, generating and modifying ideas; and
- the capability of rethinking ideas to meet one's immediate needs and the challenges of the current task and/or situation (Pressley & Afflerbach, 1995).

These competencies are heavily language-based, language dependent, and thus underscore the critical component of language instruction that involves reading/e-texting strategies instruction. In the twenty-first century, not only does this instruction entail those competencies outlined by Pressley and Afflerbach, they must include attention drawn to and strategies discussed for e-texts' various forms and functions and the most efficient way to derive meaning from them.

In e-text, regardless of the visual order or arrangement of what one sees, the mind actively works at detecting its own links, groupings, matches, and inter-relatedness, *to make sense, to make meaning*.

We thrive in information-thick worlds because of our marvelous
and everyday capacities to select, edit, single out, structure,

highlight, group, pair, merge, harmonize, synthesize, focus organize, condense, reduce, boil down, choose, categorize, catalog, classify, list, abstract, scan, look into, idealize, isolate, discriminate, distinguish, screen, pigeonhole, pick over, sort, integrate, blend, inspect, filter, lump, skip, smooth, chunk, average, approximate, cluster, aggregate, outline, summarize, itemize, review, dip into, flip through, browse, glance into, leaf through, skim, refine, enumerate, glean, synopsize, winnow the wheat from the chaff, and separate the sheep from the goats.
(Tufte, 1990, p.50)

All this to say that e-texting, like reading, requires an active mind: the difference lies in the shape and shaping of that action. Indeed we have moved from being *homo logens* (the symbol user) to *homo proteus* (the shapechanger).

homo logens　　　　　　　　**homo proteus**

Even more so than with print, e-texting requires that its readers continually pose questions about its origins, its voice, and its agenda. Who is the author and for whom is he or she writing? Like print, e-texting also requires that the reader exercise responsibility in the face of the larger public good. Traditional yardsticks for civility, protocols for civil discourse, can and should be applied to e-texts just as they are to print. These issues are even more immediate and critical in intercultural contexts where the norms of the target and native cultures can vary. Language learners are shapers, not accepters, of meaning in their own and in a new language and culture. For this they need not only support and guidance, but explicit instruction in essential e-competencies.

identify	replay/reenact
assemble	link
move	trace
post	track
relay	trail

determine credibility of source
determine the agenda of the author(s)
utilize sophisticated search skills
master terms/interrelatedness of terms
make e-texts one's own versus blind appropriation

Essential e-competencies

In addition, learners need to be versed in the grammar of visual design: how multimodal elements combine to express meaning. Much of this knowledge comes from experiences with television, magazines, newspapers, and visual advertisements. As discussed in Chapter 2, being target-language conversant in the types of genres and rhetorical structures that are used in particular media can facilitate language acquisition on a number of fronts: finding voice, taking charge, and critical information selection and processing. Moreover, a facility with the metadiscourse of multimedia can support the understanding of cultural and dialectical differences and aid language learners in choosing the right communication strategies for the particular audiences that they are likely to encounter in target language telecommunications environments and elsewhere.

    The implications for these differences for reading and e-texting in general, and reading and e-texting in a second language in particular, are many. It is ultimately up to the practitioner to notice, consider, and choose to exploit such differences in the instructional process in such a way that is germane to her particular context. Perhaps the most globally exploitable aspect of various forms of electronic texts is the positive Affect that engagement with these forms can stimulate and sustain. E-texts in the middle (*mediating*) position can serve to diffuse tension, support and sustain active engagement, stimulate thought and Communication that truly matters to learners, and generally motivate the kinds of 'minds-on' activity that bespeaks of powerful learning. Indeed, the motivational aspect of electronic texts for instruction has been their most consistent clarion call from all sectors – research, practitioners, and industry.

E-LITERACY AND CLASSROOM DISCOURSE

Experienced teachers have built an extensive verbal and non-verbal repertoire of moment-by-moment methods of supporting learning. They do so around any number of objects and concepts in the classroom environment as the central activity for student learning. Electronic texts possess some features that are unique and, as such, uniquely exploitable by teachers both in terms of designing and supporting instructional activity. For example, you can orally annotate both on-screen and off-screen visual material as learners use these in various tasks. What makes on-screen material different is its physical feature of mystery and potentiality; one is never thoroughly certain "what will happen if – ." This unpredictability of e-text is one of many characteristics that renders it a dialogic tool *par excellence.*

Many claims have been made that the use of e-texts in language instruction has the potential to fundamentally alter the dynamics of classroom discourse. There are affordances that accompany the unique features of the medium that, when carefully exploited in tandem with good teaching, can go beyond simply supporting the language learning process to augmenting them. In our mediated model of technologies use, talking with, through, and around e-texts is a powerful means of second language and literacy learning. Consider some of the features that are unique to e-text and some of the learning-productive talk and activity they can afford:

Pubicness
Whatever happens on a computer screen (one that is larger than 13 inches, that is) is public activity. Letters, words, images, their spatial and semiotic relationships, and the actions exerted on them are all in a public domain. The first major affordance of this characteristic is that instructors and students can 'talk off' the material. Teachers can get an immediate, visual take on learner process and support, scaffold, and further that process accordingly. Moreover, the public nature of e-texting is powerful for those learning an additional language in terms of *Display Literacy* – learners demonstrating that they can think and do in the target language.

Instability
Whereas the public nature of e-text affords discourse that refers directly to what is seen on the screen, the instability of what is seen and not seen on the screen also stimulates talk. The difference with talk concerning the unseen and unstable is that it is characterized by speculation and

conjecture. This kind of discourse is easily orchestrated by virtue of e-texts' instability.

Malleability
Discourse that is anchored to changes to e-text on the screen is a natural outgrowth of classroom computing. E-texts can be sized, shaped, colored, moved, linked, deleted, and augmented through additional modalities. Public changes can be questioned, commented on, and negotiated with others. Like instability, malleability lends itself to discourse that is often hypothetical (*if you* ____, *that will* ____) and, as such, makes for powerful practice thinking, reacting, and responding in the target language.

Multimodalities
For language learning this is a feature *sine qua non*. If a learner does not comprehend the target language in one modality, there are supports in others – textual, visual, aural. Such reinforcing referents can scaffold comprehension, are excellent Forms to which teachers can draw learner attention, and can stimulate and support productive talk and activity.

Anarchy
This very special quality of e-text has some powerful implications for teaching and learning language and literacy. First, in classroom contexts, it is almost always the teacher who is in control. When a learner is working on a computer with control over the mouse and keyboard, the learner becomes the one in control. As such, she is in a position of initiating and ending conversations (turning away and/or ignoring an interlocutor is somehow acceptable when engaged in learning with a computer). The fact that she can initiate and control the topic of conversation is a rare, but highly desirable aspect in the language learning process. Secondly, because the learner can exercise her will, satisfy her curiosities, and make independent decisions (with or without scaffolding and assistance), she is in an affective state that can be construed as being supportive to the language learning process.

MODELS AND SCAFFOLDS

In conjunction with the instability and malleability of visual referents on the computer screen, teacher and peer talk can be orchestrated to provide concrete, highly referenced, highly motivated, engaged language practice. Teachers can initiate learners into membership in e-text-based discourse communities by modeling and encouraging use of the language that accompanies thought about and use of the electronic texts that mediate their learning. One example of this is a Spanish teacher who put the language of cooperating around the computer through the chunquing process. By chunquing the language needed to work in tandem on a multimedia language learning assignment, she derived a list of some forty expressions in Spanish that she explicitly taught, modeled, and reinforced during computer-based activities. After only a few weeks, of this first year, first semester class, she noted that her students were using these expressions quite easily not only while working around the computers, but also during other off-line activities! This practice became so successful that she expanded this list and incorporated credit for using these expressions in individual assessment portfolios (Meskill et al., 1996).

Learner talk around computers generally indicates a great deal of topic control on the part of language learners, something very unique to most language instruction. This implies the dissolution of traditional forms of authority whereby the teacher is the determiner and sustainer of topics for talk (Meskill & Mossop, 2000). In this way, authority and authenticity become defined by and made part of a community of learners. These are no longer external, arbitrarily determined constructs of power and authority. On the contrary, e-text contexts of use can be designed to promote learner autonomy, empowerment, and unprecedented opportunity for anchored, meaningful talk. Such contexts can open new doors to new ways of thinking and thinking well about and through the complex problems of the contemporary world and articulating these using target language writing and speech

One of the key elements for an effective e-text for language acquisition context is the purposeful fluidity of learning activity that moves from off-computer to on-computer back to off-computer. We know that for student language learning with e-text to be meaningful, this learning must be 'set up' in advance of working with the computer. As such, it must begin away from the machine where goals, procedures, learning foci, and the language needed to successfully undertake the online work are worked through as a group. Learners then move to be in front of and/or around the computers to accomplish the socially construed and well-anchored tasks they have been assigned. While this work is going on, the focal language for the task is encouraged by the nature of the task itself, the peer interaction that has been designed into the task and its procedures, and by the instructor. Effectively designed e-text learning communities are distinguished by on-demand, moment-by-moment instructor modeling, scaffolding, and target language support. In its role as catalyst for human communication/language acquisition, the machine stimulates, supports, and services the immediate needs of the learning community.

SUMMARY

There are numerous important differences between e-texts and the more familiar print form, differences that clearly carry implications for language and literacy development. However, print form and electronic texts should never be considered in competition or opposition. Each form provides a unique experience and the potential for linguistic and intellectual growth. With print literacy, meaning is seen as building between a text and a reader through transaction. Likewise, transacting with electronic texts can be viewed as constructing meaningful experiences and knowledge between what appears on a screen, an e-texter, and others.

Our evolving e-literacy might be construed as the control we exert over representational forms used in successful communication. The range of available forms with which we can do this, and the ease and facility contemporary tools afford us for these tasks continues to expand. Our responsibility as language educators is to continue to design many-faceted pedagogies that support the appropriate, simultaneous mastery of language and e-literacy.

Activities

COMING TO TERMS...

Draft your definition of the term "electronic literacy." Now review the definitions at the beginning of Chapter 1. Do these in any way alter or enhance the definition you drafted above?

Literacy: It's not apolitical

All literacies carry both cognitive and sociopolitical consequences. They are never culturally, politically, nor economically neutral. Underlying all is what a given group understands as being valued and good about human thought and activity. As was discussed in Chapter 2, on a computer screen, as on television, there is no question that the vast majority of material has been, in one way or another, "flavored by exported American economic and cultural values" (Hawisher & Selfe, 2000, p. 5). The preponderance of U.S. forms and functions in computer software and the Internet are laden with messages tied not to the global community, but to values, interests, and agendas which become insidiously and seductively appropriated as global standards.

The flip-side consists of the Internet representing an outlet *sine qua non* for the otherwise disempowered to take action and be heard. Close examination of work by the culturally and economically disenfranchised, however, reveals that the forms and functions used for representation are indeed "flavored" by Western elite/consumer influences. Whether or not this deflates and devalues their messages is a subject highly contested in postmodern theory. If opening up discourse opportunities carries with it constraints in the forms and function available to the interlocutors (e.g. these are appropriated from an evolving 'mainstream set' and are, specifically, sense of author[authority]ship, visual layout, use of visuals, capitalist and democratic agendas of representation, and the like), is it indeed a matter of "opening up"? Even though the 'reader' and 'writer' of e-texts is hypothetically free of constraints on self-expression, can those conventions of representation in electronic environments be considered neutral? Or does their value-ladenness accompany their appropriation and recycling? Therein lies at least one fallacy associated with the mythological "Global Village" – the social/psychological narrative that pretends that the magic of technology will give equal voice to all the world's peoples. Those learning an additional language need to understand their own and the target culture's positioning in terms of "the village myth."

There is some growing belief that, with so much information, meaning is rapidly diminishing. If one examines call-in talk shows and political debates, for example, it is clear that there is no longer meaningful communication going on. Rather, these forums are designed to broadcast and manipulate the desires of their audiences. Likewise, the Internet has become a gauntlet of schlock one must traverse to arrive at what one is seeking. Discuss whether and why this kind of inquiry can and should be an integral part of language learning activity involving media and technology.

Who's that talking?
More advanced learners can certainly benefit from engaging topics and issues for which multiple perspectives can be sought via telecommunications. One of the major affordances of telecommunications is the possibility of exploring a topic or issue from a wide range of perspectives. Instant access is available to a wide range of perspectives and the continuum of discourses that constitute human society. Assign a topic or controversial issue and have learners collect at least three distinct voices (points of view) on it. Have them ask the following about the texts they locate:

- from where are these texts generated

- who is speaking
- for whom and to whom is the author(s) speaking?
- rate on a class-devised continuum of authenticity

Conventions: Nothing New Under the Sun?

Characteristics of electronic text are more often than not born out of The Media. Current conventions for displaying, organizing, and responding to electronic texts have their roots in newspapers, magazines, radio, books, and, more perhaps than ever, television. When you consider the purpose and agenda of these popular media, most often it is to entertain. The essence of entertainment is to address, capture, and retain our interest. One surefire method of doing so is through playfulness. A great deal of popular media can be characterized by its playfulness through jokes, double entendres, language play, verbal duels, songs, little fictions, puzzles, etc. In your experience, has any of this playfulness been appropriated by electronic texts?

Desk Potatoes?

The phenomenal growth in access to and information on the Internet has brought its own frets—mostly along the same lines as television—that hours spent cruising the web are hours not spent in social, physical, or reading activity. Instead of couch potatoes, we'll be a planet of desk potatoes. In short, our 'new literacy' will render us non-physically social. Have you stumbled across any evidence of this in your own experience? Recall The Media Addict in Chapter 2 who found her own technology-laden L2 laboratory in her living room a more comfortable place than the real world. Is this a risk for L2 learners with computers in their homes?

Total Physical Response

This low-level activity involves learners becoming familiar with hardware and operating system fundamentals and the target language words that refer to them. There are numerous possible variations of having learners follow TPR-like instructions to such as identifying parts, opening or saving a file, or moving text around the screen. Try designing a simple set of TPR commands for your learners that direct them to parts of the machine and functionality of the machine's operating system.

What we do, what to teach...

James Sosnoski (1999) listed actions he found himself employing while e-texting, or what he calls "hyper-reading." He published this list as an invitation to others to match what he describes as his experiences to their own. I have compared these actions with what I find myself doing and invite you to do the same. In addition, I have made a parallel list of implications for teaching and learning language and literacy to accompany each of these actions. I invite you to do the same for a group L2 students, real or imagined.

Filtering and selecting
Sosnoski reports that he finds himself *filtering* and *selecting* more frequently when hyper-reading than when print reading. This greater amount of selectivity translates into greater relevance-making of the material one encounters and chooses to attend to. But, he argues, it does not render the process or the outcome more subjective and personal. It was the author(s) of the search engines and the sites themselves that selected *what* and *how* he ended up filtering.

    I, too, find myself filtering quite a bit when e-texting, wondering particularly what the thought or logic was behind keyword selection and links. I am often hyper-aware of the design and agenda behind what I see on the screen just as I am with print. I check the URL for the source institution the document or author is affiliated with, and if it is an official affiliation of some kind.

Teaching Filtering
When children are taught to read books, they are signaled to the publication information on the inside page. They are cued to the date and place of publication and to gauge the age of the author. Academicians do this for all texts as a matter of course. The judgements made and schema against which the text gets read consequently influence the reading in many discrete ways. This basic level of filtering can be taught as part of e-texting to L2 learners where consideration of the source is perhaps more critical to full comprehension. Have students read portions of e-text (software or web sites) without considering its authorship. Have them provide a brief oral or written summary. Repeat the activity, but include a "filtering' portion where strategies for determining and understanding the source/authorship is included. Have students read those same passages with the source knowledge as background. They can then compare and contrast their original interpretations and reactions to the newer, more informed ones.

Filming, i.e. "cinetizing"
When we read a book, in conjunction with the printed word, we invoke a range of associative images, mostly 'original' concoctions in the theater of our minds. Sosnoski claims that electronic texts provoke another genre of associative images, these from our visual culture. Stills and motion pictures that are part of electronic texts, he argues, require conceptual links to similar, visual associations to truly make sense. To test his hypothesis, have your students "talk aloud" as they navigate/read the visuals that are integrated in electronic texts. Have them compare and contrast their associations with those they make while reading print.

APPENDIX: FOR FURTHER READING

Cummins, J. and Sayers, D. (1997) *Brave New Schools: Challenging Cultural Illiteracy through Global Learning Networks.* New York: St. Martin's Press.

Hawisher, G. and Selfe, C. (2000) *Global literacies and the world-wide web.* New York: Routledge.

Warschauer, M. (1999) Electronic literacies: Language, culture, and power in online education. Mahwah, NJ: Lawrence Erlbaum.

Epilogue

Putting it All Together

Language teaching professionals make creative use of objects and tools meant for different, sometimes very different, applications. They do so by assessing, combining, and manipulating them for specific pedagogical purposes. The instructional uses for media and technologies discussed in the preceding chapters are certainly no exception. These principled examples of teaching craft demonstrate that no amount of engineering on the part of government, business, and educational administrations can alter the fact that a mainstay of good language teaching is making use of what is immediately available and that makes sense *to the moment*. After all, language classes consist primarily of human communication, and materials and methods that effectively support it must be flexible and responsive to the chaos and complexity of human interaction.

The craft of teaching language often means coming up with a theme, topic, or concept that both has meaning for, and motivates a specific group of learners. From initial idea to the actual in-class debrief on an integrated activity, the teaching professional goes through a number of iterative and creative steps and processes. Understanding well the vast resources represented by media and technology, their unique characteristics, and potential complementary roles in second language acquisition, is one facet of a much larger endeavor: designing and implementing instruction that makes sense for a given group of individuals. From exploiting a piece of aural text in order to model and reinforce a grammatical structure to orchestrating complex group interaction with, through, and around an e-text, the language activity design considerations are much the same: What are the special attributes of this medium that support my goals? How can these best be exploited?

System or Chaos?

Teaching with media and technologies can be viewed as being closely aligned with art. The ethos of the learning experience flows through and around a mediating object, an object that inspires and supports the human enterprise of making meaning and broadening one's understandings of the world in dialogue with it. Media and technologies can serve as a lubricant that greases the wheels of learning activity and support its accompanying discourse. Unfortunately, a good deal of technology appropriation takes place mindful of neither the nature of the language learning enterprise nor of the supportive roles and features of media and technologies in that enterprise. Too often, cosmetic adoptions of media and technologies take place: an institution procures machines, develops a rationale for having purchased them, and uses them minimally, if at all, in ways that make local pedagogical sense. In part, this blind appropriation trend is due to prevailing myths regarding things "language" and things "technological." One of the most prevalent and powerful of these myths is the myth of salvation: for any problem, there is a solution; some people learn languages easily and well, others do not; all we need do is invent the right 'technology' and the problem will be solved – we will be saved. While this myth influences many aspects of contemporary existence, it is especially tenacious in the education sector where easily identifiable problems in need of solutions abound: low achievement, need for positive publicity, appeasing stakeholders, and the like.

In the near and distant future, we will no doubt continue to equate the technological with the wondrous. Indeed, there's little doubt that wondrous technologies that will both augment and detract from human civilization are being and will continue to be developed. If our world is to indeed stay 'ours,' it remains our responsibility as educators to assure that we and our learners make good, thoughtful use of these wonders in our quest to retain and enhance our humanity, not dummy down to the agendas of those who would use technology to exploit. Where enormous optimism is typically attached to things technological, no technology will ever come near to attaining the infinitely generative and creative capacity of human language. Learning additional languages will only happen through the efforts of, and interaction with others. Regardless of the endless supply of hype and exuberance about new technologies, the enduring premises and practices of excellent language practitioners will prevail.

References

Al-Sa'Di, R. A., & Hamdan, J. M. (2005). "Synchronous online chat" English: Computer-mediated communication. *World Englishes, 24*(4), 409-424.

Anderson, R., Shirely, L, Wilson, P. and Fielding, L. (1986) Interestingness of children's reading material. In R. Snow & M. Farr (Eds.) *Aptitude, learning and instruction: Vol. 3: Cognitive and affective process analyses*. Hillsdale, NJ: Erlbaum.

Bowen, D., Madsen, H. and Hilferty, A. (1985) *TESOL techniques and procedures*. New York: Newbury House.

Boysson-Bardies, B. de (1999) *How language comes to children: From birth to three years*. Cambridge, MA: MIT Press.

Braine, G. (1997) Beyond word processing: Networked computers in ESL writing classes. *Computers and Composition, 14*, 45-58.

Breen, M. and Candlin, C. (1980) The Essentials of a communicative curriculum in language teaching. *Applied Linguistics* 1, 89-112.

Brown, G. (1994) Modes of understanding. In G. Brown, K. Malmkjaer, A. Pollitt, and J. Williams (Eds.) *Language and understanding*. New York: Oxford University Press.

Brown, H.D. (1994) *Teaching by principles*. Englewood Cliffs, NJ: Prentice Hall Regents.

Brown, J., A. Collins, and P. Duguid. (1989) Situated cognition and the culture of learning. *Educational Researcher, 18*, 32-42.

Bruner, E. (1983) Opening up Anthropology. In Bruner (Ed.) *Text, play, and story: The construction and reconstruction of self and society*. Washington, DC: American Ethnological Society.

Chomsky, N. (1986) *Knowledge of language*. New York: Praeger.

Cohn,E. (1981) France wants active young televiewers. *Television and children 4*, 29-42.

Connor, S. (1989). *Postmodern culture*. New York: Basil Blackwell.

Cosmides, L. and Tooby, J. (1992) Cognitive adaptations for social exchange. In J. Barkow, J. Tooby, & L. Comides (Eds) *The adaptive mind: Evolutionary psychology and the generation of culture*. New York: Oxford University Press.

Cuban, L (1986) *Teachers and machines: The classroom use of technology since 1920.* New York: Teachers College Press.

Cummins, J., Bismilla, V., Chow, P., Cohen, S., Giampapa, F., Leone, L., Sandu, P. & Padma, S. (2005). Affirming identity in multicultural classrooms. *Educational Leadership, 63*(1), 38-43.

Cummins, J., Brown, K., & Sayers, D. (2007). *Literacy, technology, and diversity: Teaching for success in changing times.* Boston, MA: Pearson Education, Inc.

Dale, E. (1969) *Audio-visual methods in teaching.* NY: Holt, Rinehart & Winston.

Doughty, C. and Williams, J. (Eds) (1998) *Focus on form in classroom second language acquisition.* New York: Cambridge University Press.

Dunkel, P. (1991) Listening in the native and second/foreign language: Toward an integration of research and practice. *TESOL Quarterly, 25*(3), 431-457.

Federal Communications Commission. (2009). *FCC Consumer Advisory: Closed captioning for digital television (DTV).* Washington, D.C. Retrieved February 20, 2009, from http://www.fcc.gov/cgb/consumerfacts/dtvcaptions.html.

Finkelstein, J. (2006). *Learning in real time: Synchronous teaching and learning online.* San Francisco, CA: Jossey-Bass.

Fiske, J. (1987) *Television culture.* New York: Routledge.

Friend, T. (1998) Laugh Riot. *The New Yorker*, Sept. 28:79

Goldman, M. (1996) If you can read this, thank TV. *TESOL Journal, 6*(2), 15—18.

Grice, H. (1975) Logic and conversation. in P. Cole and J. Morgan (Eds) *Syntax and Semantics*, Volume *3: Speech Acts.* New York: Academic Press.

Gunawardena, C. and Zittle, F. (1997) Social presence as a predictor of satisfaction within a computer-mediated conferencing environment. *The American Journal of Distance Education. 11*(3), 8-26.

Guyer, C. (1999) Into the next room. in G. Hawisher and C. Selfe (Eds) *Passions, pedagogies and 21st century technologies.* Logan, UT: University of Utah Press.

Hawisher, G. and Selfe, C. (2000) *Global literacies and the world-wide web.* New York: Routledge.

Higgins, (1988) *Language, learners and computers.* New York: Longman.

Hymes, D. (1972) On communciative competence. In J. Pride and J. Holmes (Eds) *Sociolinguistics.* Harmondsworth: Penguin Books.

Joyce, M. (1999) Beyond next before you once again: Repossessing the renewing electronic culture. In G. Hawisher and C. Selfe (2000

Johnson, M. (1987) *The body in the mind: The bodily basis for meaning, imagination and reason.* Chicago: Chicago University Press.

Kramsch, C. (1993) *Context and culture in language teaching.* New York: Oxford University Press.

Krashen, S. (1994) The pleasure hypothesis. *Georgetown University Round Table on Languages and Linguistics 1994.* Washington DC: Georgetown U. Press.

Krashen, S. (1985) *The input hypothesis: Issues and implications.* New York: Longman.

Kurzweil, R. (1999) *The age of spiritual machines.* New York: Penguin Books.

Losanov, G. (1978) *Suggestology and outlines of Suggestopedy.* New York: Gordon and Breach.

Lowes, J. (1990) *The road to Xanadu: A study in the ways of the imagination.* Princeton, NJ: Princeton University Press.

McLaren, P., Hammer, R., Sholle, D. and Reilly, S. (1995) *Rethinking media literacy: A critical Pedagogy of representation.* New York: Peter Lang.

Meskill, C. (1999) Computers as tools for sociocollaborative language learning. In K. Cameron (Ed.) *CALL: Media, design and applications.* Lisse: Swets & Zeitlinger.

Meskill, C. (1998) Commercial television and the limited English proficient child: Implications for language development. In K. Swan, C. Meskill, and S. DeMaio (Eds). *Social learning from broadcast television.* Cresskill, NJ: Hampton Press.

Meskill, C. (1996) U.S. Television and Non-native Speakers of English: Sociocultural and Sociolinguistic Issues. ERIC document # ED394329.

Meskill, C. (1993) ESL and multimedia: A study of the dynamics of paired student discourse. *System. 21*, 323-341.

Meskill, C. (1992) Off-screen talk and CALL: Role of the machine/participant. *Computer-assisted English Language Learning Journal, 3*(1), 1-9.

Meskill, C. (1990) Where in the world of English is Carmen Sandiego? *Journal of Games and Simulations, 21*(4) 457-460.

Meskill, C. and Jiang, M. (1996) Multimedia and language learning: A study of features that support off-screen communication practice. in Carlson, D. and Makedon, F. (eds) *Educational Multimedia and Hypermedia*. Charlottesville, VA: Association for the Advancement of Computing in Education.

Meskill, C. and Mossop, J. (2000) Electronic texts and English as a second language. *TESOL Quarterly 34*(3), 585-592.

Meskill, C., Mossop, J. and Bates, R. (2000) Bilingualism, cognitive flexibility, and electronic texts. *Bilingual Research Journal, 23*(2 & 3).

Meskill, C., Mossop, J. & Bates, R. (1999) *Electronic texts and English as a second language Environments*. Albany, NY: National Research Center on English Learning and Achievement.

Meskill, C., Shea, P., Sasson, P. and Jiang, M. (1996) Researching communicative aspects of multimedia technology for Language Instruction. *Leveraging Learning-Using and Affording Technology SUNY Faculty Access to Computing Technology Conference Proceedings*.

Meskill, C. & Swan, K. (1997) Roles for multimedia in the response-based literature classroom. *Journal of Educational Computing Research, 15*(3), 217-239.

Mildenberger, K. (1962) Problems, perspectives, and projections. *International Journal of American Linguistics, 28*(1), 168-172.

Miller, G. A. (1956), *The Magical Number Seven, Plus or Minus Two: Some Limits on our Capacity for Processing Information*. Psychological Review, *63*, 81-97

Murray, D. (1995) *Knowledge machines: Language and information in a technological society.* New York: Longman.

Mydlarski, D. (1987) Cooperative computer-assisted language learning: Is it living up to its promise? *Journal of Educational Techniques and Technologies, 20,* 26-29.

National Captioning Institute (2000) www.ncicap.org/.

Oller, J. (1978) *The language teaching controversy.* Rowley, MA: Newbury House.

Papert, S. (1993) *The children's machine: Rethinking school in the age of the computer.* New York: Basic Books.

Pica, T. (1998) Second language learning through interaction: Multiple perspectives. In V. Regan (Ed.) *Contemporary approaches to second language acquisition in social context.* Dublin: University of Dublin Press.

Pica, T. and Doughty, C. (1985) Input and interaction in the communicative language classroom: a comparison of teacher-fronted and group activities. In S. Gass and C. Madden (Eds.) *Input in Second Language Acquisition,* Rowley, MA: Newbury House.

Piper, A. (1986) Conversation and the computer: A study on the conversational spin-off generated among learners of English as a foreign language working in groups. *System, 14,* 187-198.

Pressley, M. and Afflerbach, P. (1995) *Verbal protocols of reading: The nature of constructively responsive reading.* Hillsdale, NJ: Lawrence Erlbaum.

Rain Man (1988) Perf. Dustin Hoffman, Tom Cruise. MGM.

Reeves, B. and Nass, C. (1996) *The media equation.* NY: Cambridge University Press.

Remnick, D. (1999) *King of the world.* New York: Random House.

Resnick, L (1999) From aptitude to effort: A new foundation for our schools. *American Educator, Spring* (10-13), 50-51.

Richards, J. and Rogers, T. (1986) *Approaches and methods in language teaching.* New York: Cambridge University Press.

Rost, M. (1990) *Listening in language learning.* New York: Longman.

Rushkoff, D. (1996) *Media virus.* New York: Ballantine.

Sasson, P. (1996) Supporting communicative practice with multimedia. *Proceedings of 1996 Conference on Instructional Technology.* Albany: State University of New York.

Savignon, S. (1991) Communicative language teaching: State of the art. *TESOL Quarterly, 25,* 261-277.

Schmidt, R. (1995) *Attention and awareness in foreign language learning.* Honolulu: Second Language Teaching and Curriculum Center, University of Hawaii at Manoa.

Schmidt, R. and Frota, S. (1986) Developing basic conversational ability in a second language: a case study of an adult learner of Portuguese. In Day, R. (Ed*) Talking to learn: conversation in second language acquisition.* Rowley, MA: Newbury House.

Schumann, J. (1997) *The neurobiology of affect in language.* Malden, MA: Blackwell.

Skinner, B. (1968) *The technology of teaching.* New York: Appleton-Century-Crofts.

Snyder, T. and Palmer, J. (1986) *In search of the most amazing thing.* Reading, MA: Addison-Wesley.

Sosnoski, J. (1999) Hyper-readers and their Reading Engines. In G. Hawisher and C. Selfe.

Stalin, J. V. (1972) *Marxism and Problems of Linguistics.* Peoples Republic of China: Foreign Languages Press.

Stevik, E. (1976) *Memory, meaning & method: Some psychological perspectives on language learning.* Rowley, MA: Newbury House.

Thorne, S. (1999) An activity theoretical analysis of foreign language electronic discourse. PhD dissertation. University of CA, Berkely, CA.

Toffler, A. (1980) *The third wave: The classic study of tomorrow.* New York: Bantam Books.

Tufte, E. (1990) *Envisioninginformation.* Chesire, Connecticut: Graphics Press.

Tyner, K. (1998) *Literacy in a digital world: Teaching and learning in the age of information.* Mahwah, NJ: Lawrence Erlbaum Associates.

van Lier, L. (2000) From input to affordance: Social-interactive learning from an ecological perspective. In J. Lantolf (Ed.) *Sociocultural theory and language learning.* New York: Oxford University Press.

Vygotsky, L. (1986) *Thought and language.* Cambridge, MA: MIT Press.

Vygotsky, L. (1978) *Mind in society.* Cambridge, MA: Harvard U. Press.

Warschauer, M. (1996) (ed) *Virtual connections: On-line activities for networking language learners.* Honolulu: University of Hawaii Press.

Warschauer, M. (1999) *Electronic literacies: Language, culture, and power in online education.* Hillsdale, NJ: Lawrence Erlbaum.

Warschauer, M. and Meskill, C. (2000) Technology and second language teaching and learning. In J.Rosenthal (Ed) *Handbook of undergraduate second language education.* Mahwah, NJ: Lawrence Erlbaum.

Wilson, E. (1998) *Consilience: The unity of knowledge.* New York: Vintage Books.

Winograd, T. and Flores, F. (1988) *Understanding computers and cognition: A new foundation for design.* Reading, MA: Addison-Wesley.

Wood, D., Bruner, J., & Ross, G. (1976). The role of tutoring in problem solving. *Journal of Child Psychology and Psychiatry, 17*(2), 89-100.

Wylie, Laurence (1985) Communication with the French. *The French Review*, May.

Subject Index

A

analog media · 73
Archiving student work · 147, 154, 156
asynchronous communication · 141, 142, 145, 147, 154, 155, 156
audio
    analog · 107
    lab · 27, 37, 67, 81, 84, 109, 160
    teaching with · 16, 67, 75, 77, 78, 81, 84
autism · 3

B

Brain Theatre · 76, 79, 80

C

captioning, closed · 107
chat site · 169
chat sites · 139, 169
chunquing · 50, 51, 52, 53, 54, 55, 56, 57, 60, 63, 64, 65, 74, 79, 80, 103, 152, 154, 193
The Chunquing Tool · 51
collaborative learning · 40, 59, 60, 64, 74, 102, 124, 125, 135, 139, 154, 156, 159, 164
communicative competence · 8, 40, 44, 45, 69, 91, 166
Communicative Language Teaching · 39, 40, 41, 43, 44, 45, 47, 50, 59, 60, 64, 118, 122, 123
composing · 60, 76, 114, 139, 140, 141, 142, 143, 146, 149, 150, 157, 160, 173
    cubing technique · 160
Computer Assisted Language Learning · 115, 116, 117, 118, 120, 121, 123, 127, 136, 137, 138, 203, 204
Computer Mediated Communication · 149

Constructionism · 16, 42
Constructivism · 42
Critical Literacy · 22, 33
Culture learning · 2, 19, 22, 23, 24, 25, 26, 27, 28, 29, 30, 31, 32, 33, 34, 35, 36, 37, 38, 43, 44, 45, 49, 50, 51, 54, 57, 60, 61, 62, 75, 77, 91, 93, 96, 100, 103, 105, 107, 108, 157, 158, 168, 170, 173, 174, 177, 178, 180, 181, 183, 190, 195, 198, 201, 202, 203, 207

D

Direct Method · 15
Distance Learning · 151, 152
Drill and Practice · 40, 41, 78, 81, 116, 117, 118, 119, 121, 124, 135, 153

E

Electronic babysitter · 124
Electronic Literacy · 181, 182, 183, 191, 194
Electronic Mail · 139, 144, 145, 146, 169
Electronic Texts · 143, 154, 182, 183, 184, 185, 186, 187, 188, 189, 190, 191, 192, 193, 194, 195, 196, 197, 198, 199, 204
English as a second language · 3, 24, 25, 53, 57, 94, 113, 114, 126, 127, 138, 139, 146, 180, 201, 204
Errors, dealing with · 7, 46, 47, 59, 60
Exploratory Environments CALL · 120

F

Form focused instruction · 8, 9, 10, 19, 34, 36, 40, 41, 45, 47, 60, 86, 119, 127, 131, 140, 144, 152, 156, 166, 177, 183, 184, 187

G

Grammar · 15, 38, 40, 50, 108, 117, 119, 139, 190

I

Instructionism · 16
Internet · 22, 30, 77, 136, 138, 150, 151, 161, 165, 169, 170, 171, 174, 176, 178, 182, 183, 187, 194, 195, 196

J

Journals, student · 38, 86, 136, 137

K

Keyboarding · 130, 141

L

Language
  and culture · 22, 24, 27, 30, 33, 43, 44, 45, 49, 50, 62, 92, 93, 100, 105, 157, 173, 174, 178, 181, 190
  forms · 31, 142, 147
  laboratories · 81, 108, 109
Learner/Student-centered · 40, 42, 43, 87

M

Media
  multimedia · 13, 46, 124, 151, 163, 164, 165, 166, 167, 168, 169, 174, 175, 176, 177, 181, 184, 190, 193, 204, 206
  The Media · 11, 13, 21, 22, 23, 26, 27, 30, 31, 33, 34, 196, 205
Mediated Language Learning · 39, 51, 52, 57, 68, 74, 160, 184
MERLOT · 162

N

Netiquette · 143, 162

O

Off-screen Talk · 125, 126

P

Print · 95, 129, 130, 141, 143, 154, 158, 182, 184, 185, 186, 187, 188, 189, 190, 194, 197, 198

R

Repurposing · 22, 52, 63, 78, 80

S

Scaffolding · 42, 58, 60, 65, 80, 91, 152, 191, 192, 193
Screen Literacy · 182
Simulations · 83, 120, 123, 125, 127, 131, 150
Sociocognitive Approaches · 6, 40, 41, 43, 69
Sociocollaborative Context for Learning · 41, 42, 87
Software
  commercial · 167
  instructional tools · 14, 52, 61, 87, 115, 116, 121, 126, 128, 133
  native speaker · 126, 127
  non-native speaker · 117, 127
Story · 24, 36, 75, 76, 85, 95, 97, 98, 99, 100, 102, 109, 110, 114, 119, 173
Synchronous communications · 141, 147, 150

T

Talking Books · 119
Telecommunications · 13, 47, 140, 141, 145, 146, 147, 151, 152, 157, 158, 159, 163, 169, 173, 185, 190, 195
Television · 13, 22, 27, 31, 32, 34, 35, 36, 77, 91, 97, 98, 105, 109, 113, 151, 161, 178, 202
Tutorials · 119

V

VCR · 16, 24, 27, 37, 109
Video

hardware · 124, 196
literacy · 94
teaching with · 97

W

Web pages · 159
World Wide Web · 111, 136, 137, 162, 205
Writing · 14, 35, 42, 44, 48, 49, 50, 53, 56, 57, 75, 79, 81, 83, 84, 97, 140, 141, 142, 143, 145, 148, 149, 158, 161, 172, 181, 187, 189, 193, 201
Composing Online · 160
Networked · 149, 150, 160, 201

www.ingramcontent.com/pod-product-compliance
Lightning Source LLC
Chambersburg PA
CBHW071715160426
43195CB00012B/1694